GREAT PAPER
AIRPLANES

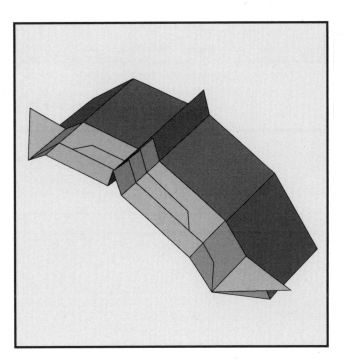

Fabulous Planes to Fold and Fly

BARNES & NOBLE BOOKS
NEW YORK

★ ★ ★

This edition published by Barnes & Noble, Inc.
by arrangement with Hugh Lauter Levin Associates, Inc.

2002 Barnes & Noble Books

ISBN: 0-7607-3480-1

M 10 9 8 7 6

Printed in Hong Kong

All material in this book has been adapted, with permission,
from *The Greatest Paper Airplanes*,
© 1998 Kitty Hawk Software, Inc.

The Greatest Paper Airplanes, from Kitty Hawk Software, Inc.,
is a recreational software program based on the theme
of flight using full interactive 3D animation to show
you how to fold extraordinary paper airplanes,

Kitty Hawk Software, Inc. is reachable at www.khs.com.

CONTENTS

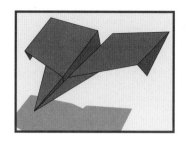

DARTS

These variations on the "schoolyard special" are fun to fold and fun to fly. They're perfect for kids of all ages.

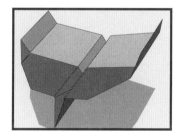

GLIDERS

Floaters and long-distance specialists, gliders perform best in a large indoor space or in the park on a calm sunny day.

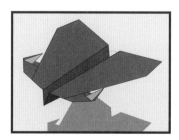

JET/BOMBER

A military craft with A-1 style, this plane will spark your imagination to create dog fights and bomb runs.

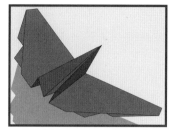

SST/STEALTH

Beautiful, sleek lines and a mach-speed look mark SST/Stealth craft as an impressive example of the art of folding paper planes.

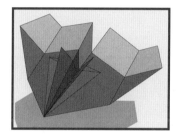

STARSHIPS

Exotic and experimental with an outer-space look, these craft push the limits of paper planes far beyond the ordinary.

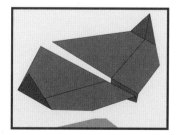

FLYING WINGS

Wide wing spans on small bodies give flying-wing aircraft great lift, enabling long, straight, and stable flight paths.

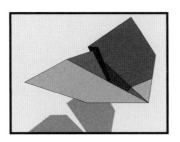

DELTA WINGS

Triangular wings with various special control surfaces give delta-wing planes an unusual look and flying style.

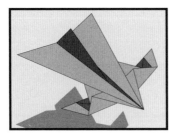

CANARD FLYERS

Forward-swept winglets allow canard flyers the extra measure of agility they need for acrobatic high-speed flights and loops.

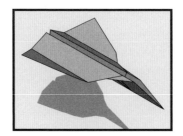

FIGHTERS

Modeled after high-performance military aircraft, fighters have the feel of real jet aircraft in combat flight maneuvers.

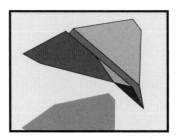

RESEARCH CRAFT

Somewhat radical and exotic in design, these new and experimental craft will test your skill as a folder and test pilot.

★ ★ ★

INTRODUCTION

TYPES OF PLANES

In this book you'll meet a number of types of paper airplanes, from long-distance specialists and wide-wing-span flyers to military, mach-speed, and outer-space craft. Whether the designs are classic or creative, you'll soon find that each plane has its own characteristic traits that make it fun to fly. Some of the planes are simple to make, such as the spiffed-up "school-yard specials" you'll find in the Dart section; others require precise folding that can take a little practice to perfect. Look for descriptions of the plane models in the Contents.

PAPER-FOLDING BASICS

Most paper airplanes fly poorly at first. The most likely reason is that the craft isn't folded tightly, meaning that the creases aren't sharp, accurate, and symmetrical. While paper folding can look almost effortless, it can be frustrating with real paper, requiring patience and practice. A plane—especially one of the more complicated models—may have to be folded several times before you get one that will fly well. Consider this a learning experience, and save your best effort (and paper) for last. And whenever you have difficulties, turn your paper so it matches the drawings, and look again. The clues you need will be there.

When you begin folding, choose light- to medium-weight paper such as copier paper, laser printer paper, and inkjet paper. Stay away from origami paper, which is colorful and easy to fold but too lightweight for top-flight performance. Origami paper also most often comes in small squares, which then must be recut to a rectangular shape for most of the craft in this book, resulting in micro-sized airplanes. Heavier paper is specified for some aircraft, but it is more difficult for a beginner to fold. Fold against a ruler, metal straightedge, or your fingernail to help ensure sharp creases. Even the first fold must be exactly right for your craft to fly well.

Most of the airplanes featured in this book require letter-size paper, although any rectangular paper will work. Remember, however, that if you're reducing the size of the paper, you will also have to proportionally reduce the typical "finger width" measurement (discussed below), used as a reference in folding some of the planes. Some planes need square paper. An easy way to make a square from a rectangle is to fold over the top edge of a rectangular sheet so it lines up with either the left or right edge. When you cut off the strip along the bottom, what's left will be perfectly square.

One of the directions you'll see over and over again in this book is to "fold the paper in half." Many times you'll need to fold the entire sheet, but other times you'll just be folding a flap or a long diagonal. Take care to fold things in half as accurately as you can. Every airplane relies on both halves being exactly the same for balance and straight flight.

Another common paper-airplane fold is called a "reverse." Reversing happens after a few key creases are established in a flat sheet. The creases are then folded in the opposite direction so that one section folds inside of another. Usually the inside section will form the plane's tail or rudder.

Most folds involve corners and edges so the creases can be made exact. Others, like the main wing fold of most planes, can only be described as "about there." Although it is imprecise, we use the width of an adult index finger as a standard reference. These folds are doubly difficult when they include many layers of paper. By trying the folds in different ways to see the effect on the airplane, you will be able to find the best way to fold each craft.

TWO FINAL TIPS: Review the construction steps completely before you begin to fold a plane, so you'll develop a sense of how the various folds come together to form the final craft. Then, during the folding process, keep your paper oriented exactly as it is shown in the illustrations. Some planes feature multiple crease lines that can become confusing if you don't use the illustration as a reference point.

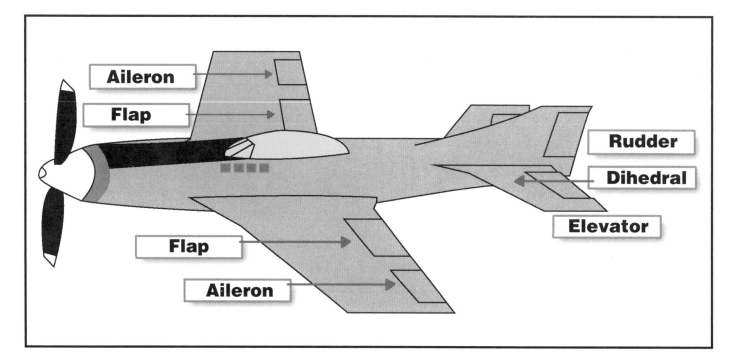

BASIC AIRPLANE TERMINOLOGY

As you build and fly the airplanes in this book, you will need to know the meanings of the words used to describe and control an airplane's flight. Real airplanes have a variety of movable surfaces that a pilot controls. Paper airplanes have fewer movable surfaces, but these surfaces are just as important to successful flight.

The critical surfaces of a plane are illustrated above. The flaps—large trailing edge sections of the wings—adjust wing area and increase lift for lower-speed landings and maneuvering. The ailerons, which are trailing edges of the wings located near the wing tips, roll the plane to the left or right for sharp turns. The rudder swings the tail back and forth for gradual turns. In the horizontal tail section there are elevators to raise or lower the nose for climbing or diving. The dihedral angle is the angle at which the wings meet the body. If an airplane's wings are completely flat (no angle), the plane will be less stable when flying and have a tendency to roll. Setting the dihedral angle is an especially critical task when flying paper airplanes. Each plane has an ideal angle, which you'll have to find by trial and error, although suggestions are offered for each of the models featured in this book.

A SHORT COURSE ON PAPER-PLANE AERODYNAMICS

The study of forces that affect an object moving through the air is called aerodynamics. The same forces that allow kites and gliders to fly also apply to real airplanes and paper airplanes. In fact, all objects are affected as they move through air or as air moves past them. Designers of airplanes, sailboats, race cars, and even buildings rely on the same principles of aerodynamics.

For airplanes, the four basic forces are *gravity, thrust, drag,* and *lift*. GRAVITY is a constant force that pulls a plane toward the ground. THRUST usually comes from an airplane's engine, but paper airplanes get their thrust from the launching throw. DRAG is the opposing force to thrust, and is caused by friction between the plane's skin and the air. Drag slows the plane, reducing the wing's ability to generate lift. Airplanes can fly only when the total lift is large enough to counteract their weight. For paper airplanes, as you will see, the "angle of attack" provides lift.

LIFT is created when moving air above a wing creates lower pressure. A Swiss mathematician, Daniel Bernoulli, discovered this effect (now called Bernoulli's Principle). You can see Bernoulli's Principle in action with a simple experiment: Tape a piece of tissue paper to the edge of a table and then blow across it. The air moving above the paper is at a lower pressure than the still air below it. This slight pressure difference will cause the paper to rise.

The same principle applies to the curved wings found on real airplanes. Air moving over the top of the wing has to travel slightly farther (and so a little faster) than the air beneath it. This causes lower pressure above the wing, which creates lift. The best wing shape for lift depends on many factors, and usually is designed using a computer and a wind tunnel for testing.

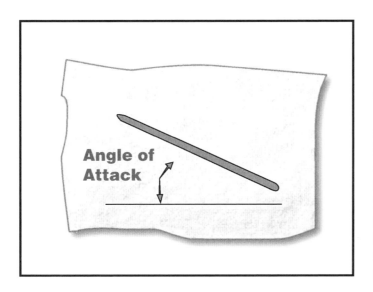

Paper airplanes don't have curved wings, so how do they fly? They use the angle of attack of their flat wings to create lift. Even though the paper wings are flat, air moving across the top surface has to travel slightly farther (and faster). Lift is generated from the same low pressure as with a curved wing, although not nearly as much lift occurs.

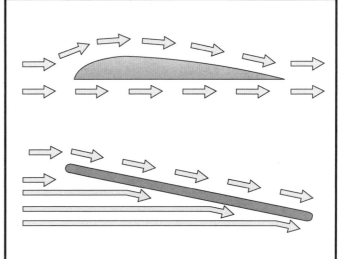

The total amount of lift also depends on air speed and wing size. Airplanes can fly only when total lift is large enough to counteract their weight. Since all the airplanes shown here weigh about the same when made of the same paper, those with smaller wings fly faster. This happens because larger wings can generate more lift even though they are flying more slowly.

FLIGHTS AND LAUNCHING

The first thing to remember when flying an airplane is to watch out for the people and pets around you. To prevent accidents, never throw a plane at somebody, even if you think he or she knows that it's coming. The sharp-nosed planes in this book carry an additional word of warning: Even though made of paper, when it's folded to a sharp point, the nose can injure upon impact, especially when it contacts a tender area such as an eye. When launching sharp-nose planes either indoors or out, be careful—and be aware that flight patterns can be erratic. To protect yourself and others, stay alert and expect the unexpected.

Regardless of the type of plane you're launching, while you're getting the hang of a new plane's ability to fly, toss it gently and at a slight upward angle. Try pushing the plane into the air, instead of throwing it—a maneuver that is the same as a throw except that you don't snap your wrist. Many times the snap of the wrist at the end of a throw will cause the plane to start its flight crooked, and the plane will fly right into the ground or spin out of control. Throw jets, darts, and higher-speed craft level and a bit harder once you've adjusted all the angles (called trimming the plane). A good way to launch a glider or a plane that floats is almost straight up. These planes will usually flip at the top of their flight paths and float a long distance before reaching the ground. An acrobatic-style craft can be thrown toward the ground. Trimmed correctly, many planes will loop-the-loop at least once before falling.

If a well-folded plane still stalls when launched, it probably has too much lift. Try adding some down elevator at the backs of the wings or tail. If the plane tends to dive, there is not enough lift and some up elevator is needed. If it rolls to the left or right, check the dihedral angles and the symmetry of the wings. If it simply flutters to the ground there is too much drag. Make sharper creases and perhaps tape down parts that impede air flow. Sometimes the addition of a paper clip or staple near the nose turns a poor flyer into a good one.

You will notice as you work your way through the folding drawings and instructions in this book that, occasionally, a specific area of a drawing has been enlarged to clarify an awkward or potentially difficult folding detail.

★ ★ ★

★ ★ ★

GREAT PAPER
AIRPLANES

★ ★ ★

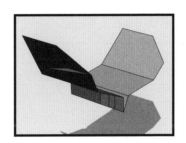

★ ★

BARRACUDA
III

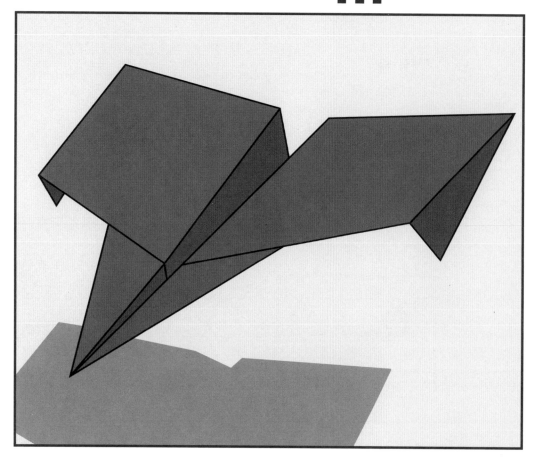

MODERATE

This dart has long-distance flight capabilities when folded and trimmed properly. Make the plane from a sheet of medium-weight letter-size paper. Take care with the folds because some can be tricky. When you're finished, launch the plane with a moderate-speed flat throw. If the dart dives for the ground, flatten the dihedral angle and try again. A very small amount of up elevator can be added if the plane continues to dive. For the most successful flight, make sure that the flaps under the wings are oriented straight up and down.

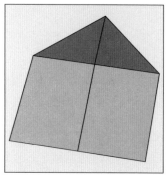

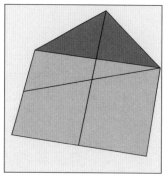

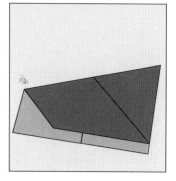

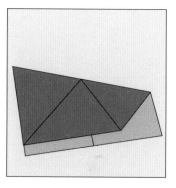

1. Fold a sheet of letter-size paper in half along its long edge. Crease and unfold. Fold the upper left corner down so the edge of the paper touches the center crease. Repeat with the upper right corner.

2. Fold down the tip of the nose so it runs along the right edge of the paper and makes a crease at the base of the folded triangle.

3. Unfold the flap that you just created.

4. Repeat the fold in the opposite direction. Fold down the tip of the nose to touch the left edge of the paper so the fold forms an X when the paper is unfolded.

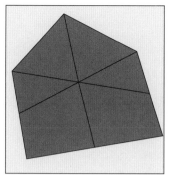

5. Unfold the flap just created and flip the paper over, keeping the nose at the top.

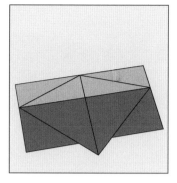

6. Fold down the nose to make a horizontal crease through the center point of the X formed in step 4. Unfold the flap.

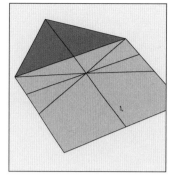

7. Flip the paper over and prepare for the next fold.

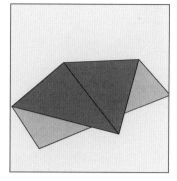

8. Grasp the ends of the horizontal crease and pull down toward you. Flattening the diagonal fold will lower the nose.

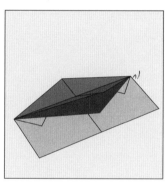

9. Fold the nose back over on itself at its widest angle.

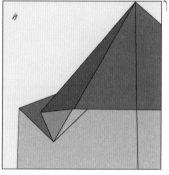

10. Fold in toward the center the left edge of the top layer from the point of the nose to the lower tip of the triangular flap. Crease the fold hard.

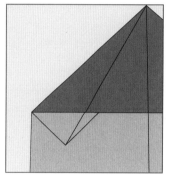

11. Unfold the flap that you just created.

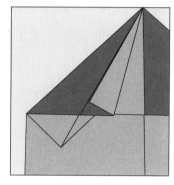

12. Fold the left center raw edge (the unfolded edge) of the nose out to the diagonal crease just created.

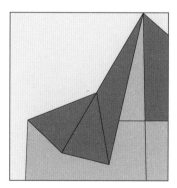

13. Fold the point on the left edge of the paper back over the existing crease. This hides the flap you just made.

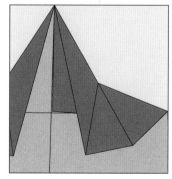

14. Repeat the same steps on the right side: Crease a fold from the nose down, ending at the lower tip of the triangular flap. The finished fold will look like the drawing.

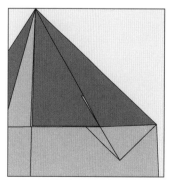

15. Unfold the flap.

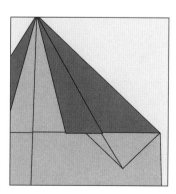

16. Fold the right center raw edge of the nose out to the diagonal crease that was just created. The top point of the crease should be at the tip of the nose.

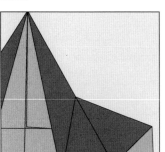

17. Fold the point on the right edge of the paper back over the existing crease. This hides the flap you just made.

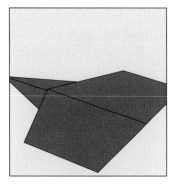

18. Flip over the plane so the flaps are underneath and the nose points away from you.

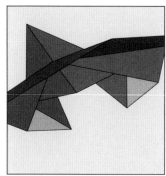

19. Lift up the bottom edge of the top paper. This will expose the flaps created during the previous steps.

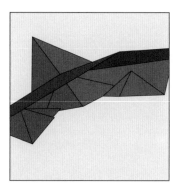

20. Fold the left triangular tip up into the plane body. Make the crease as near as possible to the other flaps. Repeat with the right triangular tip.

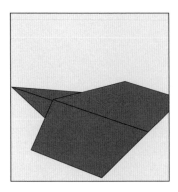

21. Press the plane flat.

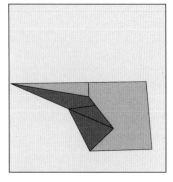

22. Fold down the plane exactly in half on the center crease. Align the wing flaps for balance. Rotate the plane so the nose points to the right and the wing flaps are up.

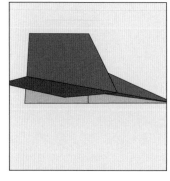

23. To crease the first wing flap, continue the bottom line of the nose flap from the nose tip through the plane end. On the left, the fold will be three fingers from the bottom.

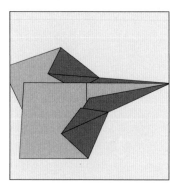

24. Flip the plane so the first wing flap is underneath and the nose points to the right.

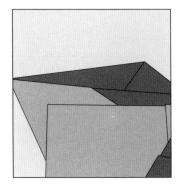

25. Fold down the outer edge of the wing flap. The tip of the triangular flap will touch the existing crease and the edge will continue the line of that crease all the way to the corner.

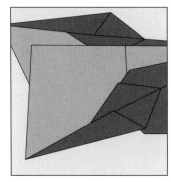

26. Repeat the folds on the other wing: Fold up the outer edge of the wing flap.

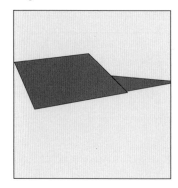

27. Fold up the second wing flap. Align the wing flaps for good balance.

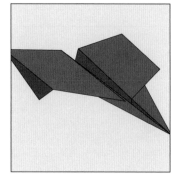

28. Open the wing flaps and adjust the angles so they're even. The wings should be flat during flight and the under-wing flaps should hang straight down.

BOTTLENOSE

MODERATE

*T*his sleek dart can be thrown hard and will travel fast, especially when constructed of medium- to heavy-weight paper. The plane isn't difficult to make, but construction does require a number of accurate folds. Launch this craft with a swift throw at just about any angle you wish. If it spirals through the air, make sure the nose is perfectly straight, the dihedral angle is definitely downward, and the wing tips are perfectly even. Because this plane can move extremely quickly, make sure to clear the area before the launch.

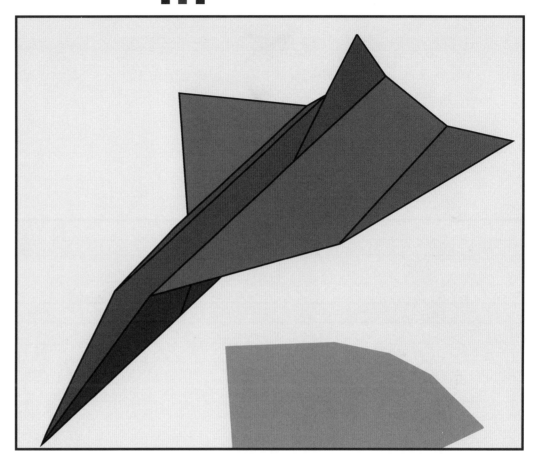

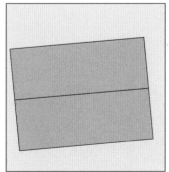

1. Start with a letter-size sheet of paper, and fold it in half along its long edge. Unfold after creasing.

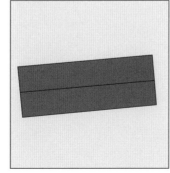

2. Fold the top edge of the paper over so the edge touches the center crease. Then fold up the bottom to the center. Rotate the paper.

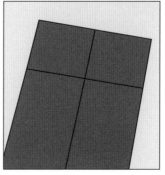

3. Fold the upper left corner down so the point touches the center crease. The edge of the fold should align with the center crease. Repeat with the upper right corner.

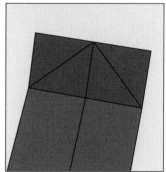

4. Fold the top edge down, creating a horizontal crease at the bottom of the flaps. Unfold the paper.

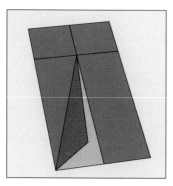

5. Crease the left wing flap.

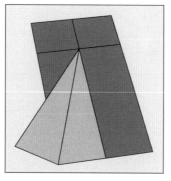

6. Run the crease between the edge of the top fold and the paper's bottom left corner.

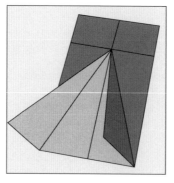

7. Crease the right wing flap in the same way as the left.

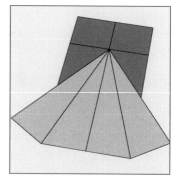

8. As with the left flap, make sure the crease aligns with the edge of the fold at the top and the right corner of the sheet at the bottom.

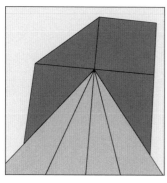

9. Fold down the upper left corner so the point touches the center crease. The bottom edge of the crease should align with the edge of the fold beneath it.

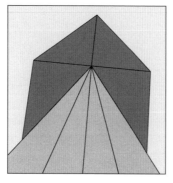

10. Fold down the upper right corner to meet the left corner, aligning the bottom edge of this fold with the fold that's underneath it.

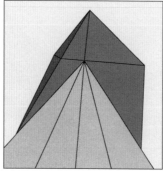

11. Fold over the point on the left edge of the nose.

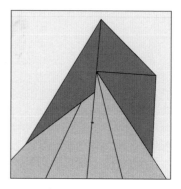

12. Make sure the fold touches the center crease.

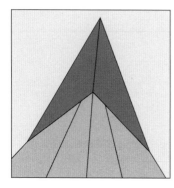

13. Fold over the point on the right edge of the nose so it follows the center crease. For good balance, it's critical to line up the folds.

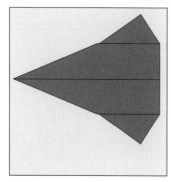

14. Flip the plane over, pointing the nose to the left.

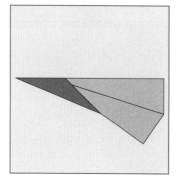

15. Fold down the plane in half along the existing center crease by bringing the top flap down.

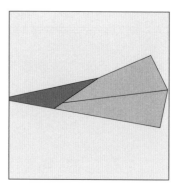

16. Flip over the plane again with the nose to the left and the wing flaps up.

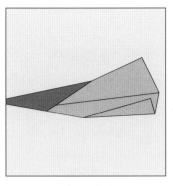

17. Crease the tail section. Start the right end of the crease about two finger widths from the base, with its left end a third of the way along the fuselage's bottom edge.

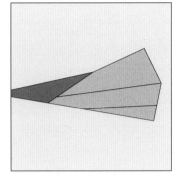

18. Unfold the tail section.

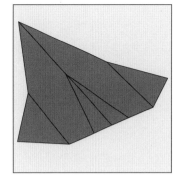

19. Flip over the plane and rotate. Unfold along the center crease.

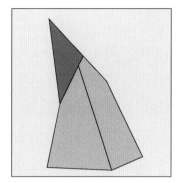

20. Put the two sides of the plane together again, using the tail section creases to fold the tail into the body. (see paragraph on reverse fold on p.5)

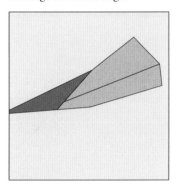

21. Hold the plane with the nose to the left and the wing flaps up.

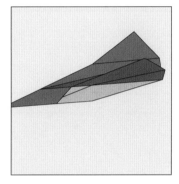

22. Make a crease for the first wing flap. The right point of the crease is the bottom left edge of the tail. The left point is about a finger width up from the base.

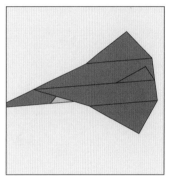

23. Make sure that the crease is even with the bottom edge of the fuselage.

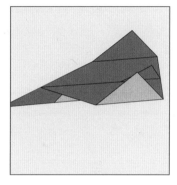

24. Fold the tip of the lower wing flap up along the existing crease.

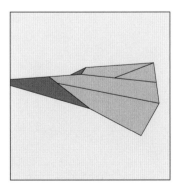

25. Roll the plane over so that the first wing flap is underneath and the nose points to the left.

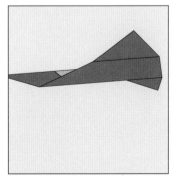

26. Make a crease for the second wing flap. Be sure to line up the wing flaps to ensure good balance.

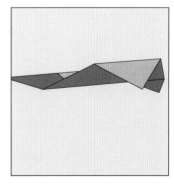

27. Fold the upper wing tip down on the existing crease. Turn over the plane.

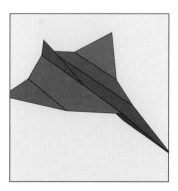

28. Open the wing flaps and make the wing angles even. Make sure that the main wing flaps have a good measure of down dihedral angle while keeping the wing tips up.

ALBATROSS

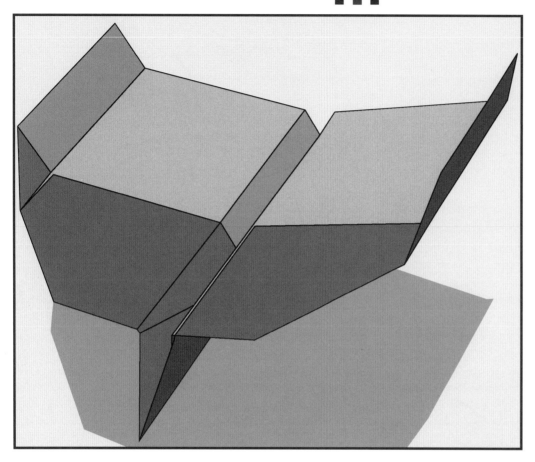

MODERATE

A good indoor craft, this glider works best when constructed of medium- to heavy-weight paper. It's not difficult to make, although you must pay attention to crafting precise folds if you want the plane to fulfill its flying potential. A piece of tape across the midsection will add stability in flight, if it's needed. Launch the Albatross with a soft throw at a slight upward angle. Harder throws will cause this craft to stall. If you notice that the plane tends to roll in flight, fine-tune the dihedral angle downward and adjust the vertical stabilizers so they're as perpendicular to the wings as you can get them.

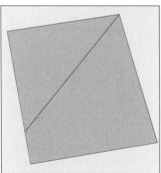

1. Starting with a letter-size piece of paper, fold down the upper left corner so the top edge lines up with the paper's right edge.

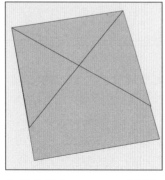

2. Unfold the paper, and fold down the upper right corner in the same way, unfolding after creasing.

3. Flip over the paper, keeping the diagonal creases toward the top.

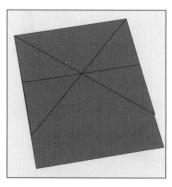

4. Fold the upper edge of the paper down to form a crease that runs through the center of the intersecting diagonal lines. Unfold.

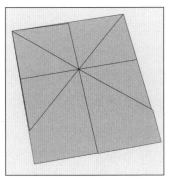

5. Flip over the paper, keeping the horizontal crease toward the top, and fold the paper in half along its long edges. Unfold after creasing.

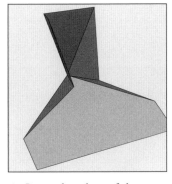

6. Grasp the edges of the horizontal crease and bring them together while pulling them down to meet the vertical crease.

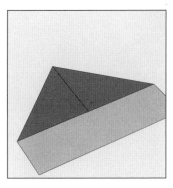

7. This results in a new flap that sticks straight up out of the plane's body. The triangular flaps lie flat.

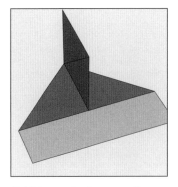

8. Pull the front points of the vertical flap down to meet the end points of the flat triangular flaps.

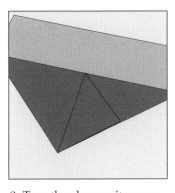

9. Turn the plane so its nose points down and slightly to the left. Fold down the right point of the right triangular flap so it touches the tip of the nose.

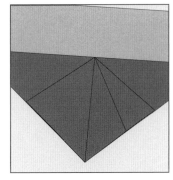

10. Fold the left point down in the same manner. Fold the right edge of the right triangular flap over so it aligns with the center crease. Unfold after creasing.

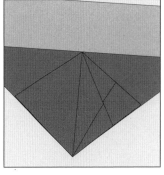

11. Fold again, bringing the right edge of the right triangular flap up to the center crease starting at the bottom point of the triangle. The left edge will align with the center crease.

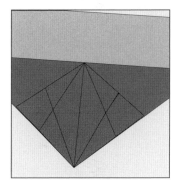

12. Unfold the crease. Repeat these folds on the left triangular flap.

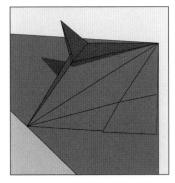

13. Turn the paper so the nose points to the right. Fold the inside edges of the two long triangular flaps to the center crease, pinching the middles together forming a new upright flap.

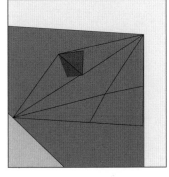

14. Swing the upright flap from side to side, pressing down hard to crease the paper.

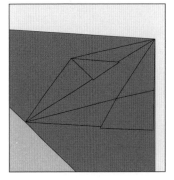

15. Fold the upright flap toward the nose tip. Then turn the plane so the nose is pointing up and to the left.

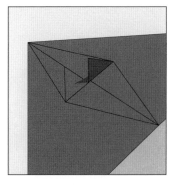

16. Repeat the fold on the opposite triangular creases to form the upright flap.

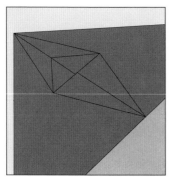

17. Press the flap toward the nose tip. Then turn the plane so the nose points down and to the right.

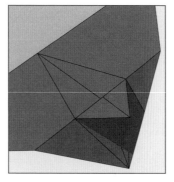

18. Fold the nose under, leaving the two upright flaps in place. Align the crease of the new fold with the crease made to fold down the upright flaps.

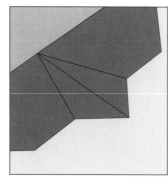

19. Press the nose firmly into the plane's main body.

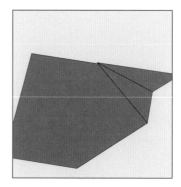

20. Fold the plane in half up along its center crease. Line up the two flaps so the plane will be balanced. Flip over the plane so the nose points to the left and the wings are up.

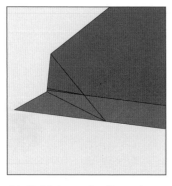

21. Fold down the first wing flap just above the nose. The crease should be even with the bottom edge of the fuselage and should be about one finger width wide.

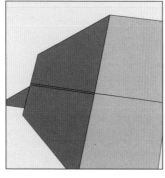

22. This is how the plane should look.

23. Flip the plane over so the first wing flap is underneath.

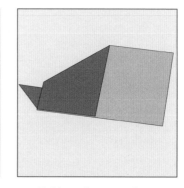

24. Fold up the second wing flap. Make sure to line up the wing flaps for good balance. Flip over the plane so the wing flaps are pointed down and the nose is to the left.

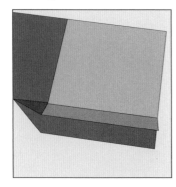

25. Fold up a vertical stabilizer on the wing tip. It should be about a finger width wide. The crease must be even and horizontal across the plane's wing tip.

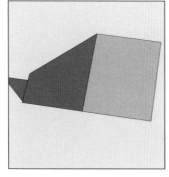

26. Flip over the plane so the wing flap with the vertical stabilizer is underneath.

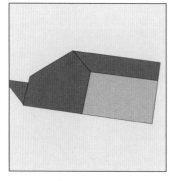

27. Fold down a stabilizer on the other wing tip. For balance, the stabilizers on each wing must be the same. Open up the wing flaps and the stabilizers.

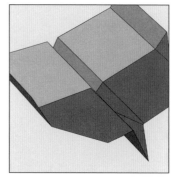

28. Adjust the dihedral angle so that it's flat or slightly downward, and make the stabilizers vertical to the wings. Add no elevator, as this will cause the craft to stall.

SEA GULL

This plane is as easy to build as it looks, but you might become confused when folding the nose section, where a number of folds are needed. Some of the folds must be constructed underneath existing folds, so in these areas follow the instructions and pictures particularly carefully. Medium- to heavy-weight paper works best for this plane. Launch the Sea Gull with a soft to medium throw, gripping the underside of the nose. This craft flies best when launched level or at a slight upward angle from a high place. A true glider that will go long distances, this plane can be a bit tempermental, so you may need to experiment a bit to get the desired flight pattern.

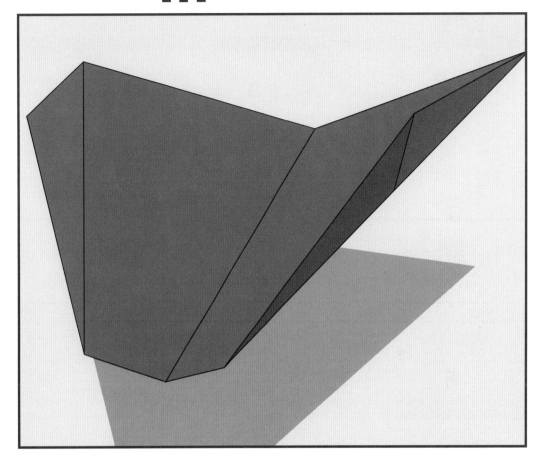

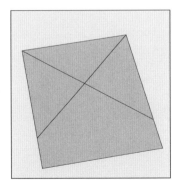

1. Fold down the upper right corner so the top edge of the paper aligns with the left side. Unfold. Repeat with the upper left corner and unfold.

2. Flip over the paper, keeping the diagonal creases toward the top. Fold down the upper corners to meet the ends of the diagonal creases.

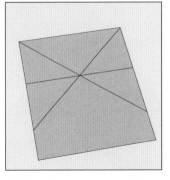

3. Turn the paper over. When folded correctly, the new crease will intersect the center point of the diagonal creases. Unfold the paper.

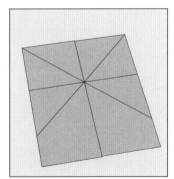

4. Fold the paper in half along its long edge. Unfold.

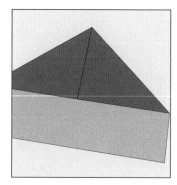

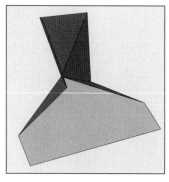

5. Pull the ends of the center crease in and down to create an upright center flap.

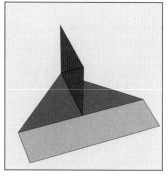

6. Re-crease the two triangular side folds so they lay flat against the plane's body.

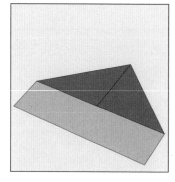

7. Pull apart the front points of the upright flap, and bring them down to overlay the flat triangular folds.

8. Fold over the top left triangular flap so its point touches the point of the opposite triangle.

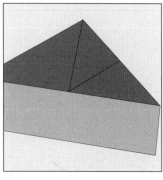

9. Fold up the flap so the right point of the triangle touches the point at the tip of the nose.

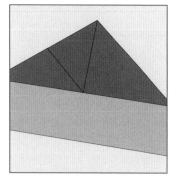

10. Fold over the new triangle onto the other side of the center line.

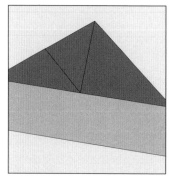

11. Fold over the large right-hand triangle so it covers the little triangle on the left. Fold the left point of the triangle so it touches the tip of the nose.

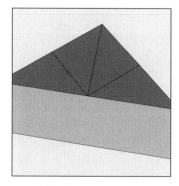

12. Fold the top triangle over to the right. You should now have a triangle on each side of the center.

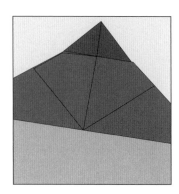

13. Fold down the nose so it hits the center crease about the width of two fingers from the top.

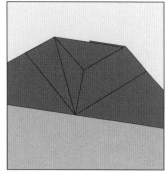

14. Fold over the left point of the larger triangle to meet the center crease at the top of the paper. Unfold after creasing.

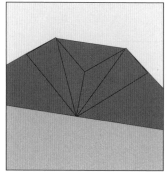

15. Repeat with the right triangle. Crease hard before you unfold the paper.

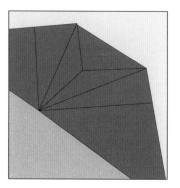

16. Turn the plane, keeping the nose up and to the right.

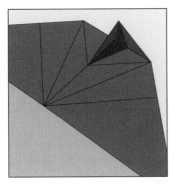

17. Open the first two layers of the small triangle at the nose to form a pocket. The pocket is exaggerated here to show the fold; the opening will be about half a finger width high.

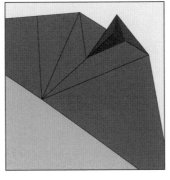

18. Carefully tuck the right point of the larger triangle into the pocket.

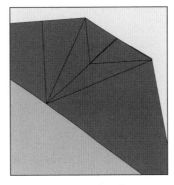

19. Press the pocket flat.

20. Rotate the plane so the nose points up and to the left.

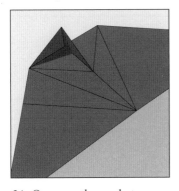

21. Open up the pocket on the left side of the plane. As before, the width is exaggerated here.

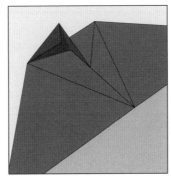

22. Insert the triangular flap of the larger triangle into the pocket of the small one.

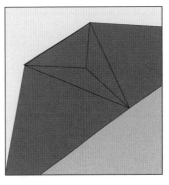

23. Press the pocket flat.

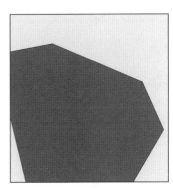

24. Flip over the plane and turn it so the nose points to the right.

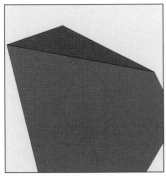

25. Crease a vertical stabilizer on the wing tip. Run the crease from the upper left corner of the wing to the edge of the nose.

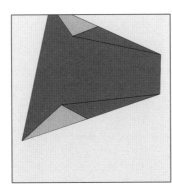

26. Crease a vertical stabilizer on the other wing.

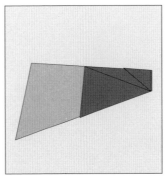

27. Fold down the plane in half along the center crease, pressing down hard. Line up the wing flaps for good balance. Open up the plane.

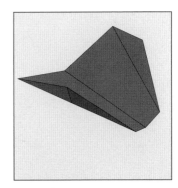

28. Set the dihedral angle flat or slightly upward. Set the stabilizers so they're about 45 degrees to the wings. Set no elevators or the craft will stall in flight.

FALCON

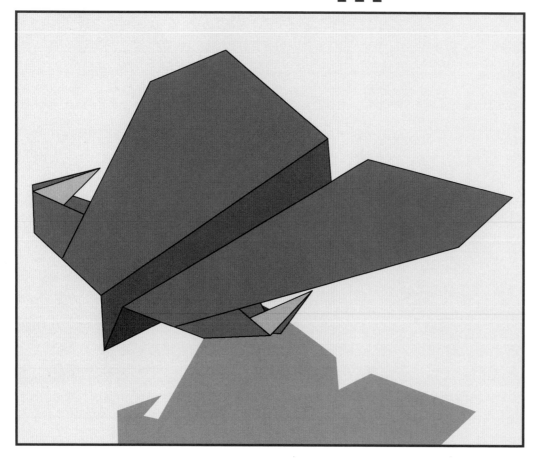

The folds in this plane are easy to construct, except for the winglet folds, which may require some interpretive fudging on your part. For best results, use medium- to heavy-weight paper. When launching, throw the Falcon at a slight upward angle. Depending on the trim, it will loop or sail for long distances. With flat wings and just a touch of up elevator, the flight path will be long and straight. By contrast, lots of up elevator will cause the plane to turn loops. And if you change the angle of the front winglets even slightly, you won't be able to predict how the plane will fly.

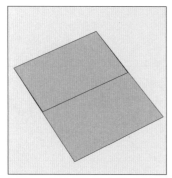

1. Crease the paper in half across its width, then unfold.

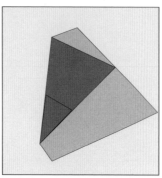

2. Fold the upper left corner to meet the end of the horizontal crease. Unfold.

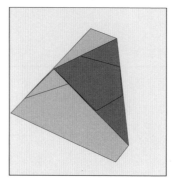

3. Fold the upper right corner to meet the end of the horizontal crease on the other side of the paper.

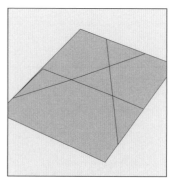

4. Completely unfold the paper and lay it flat on the work surface.

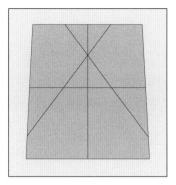

5. Crease the paper in half lengthwise and unfold.

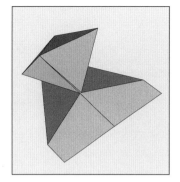

6. Grasp each end of the horizontal crease by pulling forward and down. This will create an upright flap.

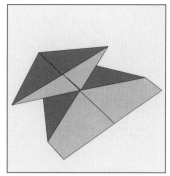

7. Grasp the front points of the flap and spread them apart while pulling them toward the work surface.

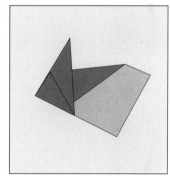

8. As you pull, the top surface will form a triangle. Press the triangle fold flat.

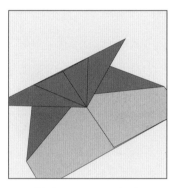

9. Fold the top triangle down at its base so the tip of the nose touches the center crease. Make a sharp crease.

10. Flip over the paper so the flaps are underneath.

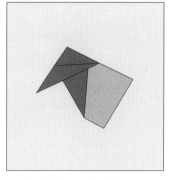

11. Fold down the plane in half along the center crease. Line up the wing flaps precisely for good balance.

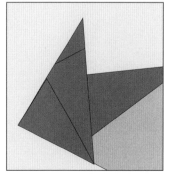

12. Flip over the plane so the wing flaps point up and the nose points left.

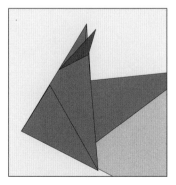

13. Fold the top point of the upper triangle down and toward the right.

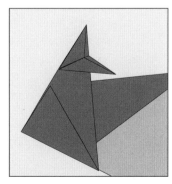

14. The dimensions of this fold aren't critical, but don't make the flap too large.

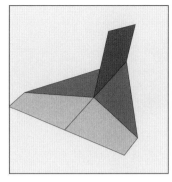

15. Unfold the flap you just created and rotate the plane as shown in the next step.

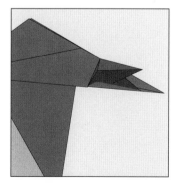

16. Pull open the two layers of the small triangle, and bring the point at the tip over and down.

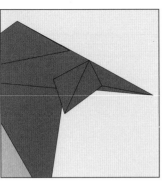

17. When you press the fold flat, you'll wind up forming two new creases.

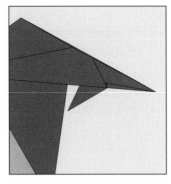

18. Fold the left point on the small triangle to the right. It will wind up covering a triangle of similar size and shape to itself.

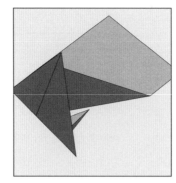

19. Flip over the paper and rotate it so the tip points down.

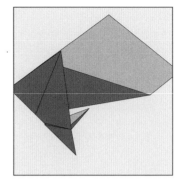

20. Fold up the point on the tip so the new crease matches the crease on the other side. Unfold the paper.

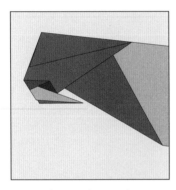

21. Pull open the two layers of the small triangle, then bring the point at the tip over and down.

22. Pressing the fold flat will produce two new creases.

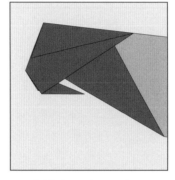

23. Fold the point on the small triangle over and down, as before. Both sides should match in size and shape.

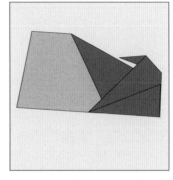

24. Rotate the plane so the wing flaps are up and the nose faces right.

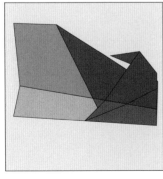

25. Fold down the first wing flap. Its right point should be about one finger width up from the bottom; its left point should be about two finger widths up.

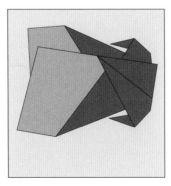

26. Flip over the plane so the first wing flap is underneath and the nose faces right.

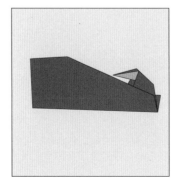

27. Fold up the second wing flap, lining it up with the first. Open up the wing flaps and adjust the wing angles so they're even.

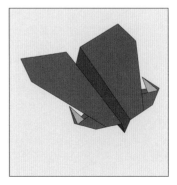

28. Set the dihedral angle flat or slightly upward. A down dihedral will cause this craft to fly upside down.

PANTHER

III

MODERATE

This neat-looking stealth bomber is a one-of-a-kind plane and flies very well when properly made. Although the construction is moderately difficult, the fun of flying this craft more than makes up for the time you'll spend to build it. For long gliding flights, launch the Panther gently from a high place. If the craft tends to always turn in the same direction, it's a sign that the plane was not made exactly the same on both sides. Twist the wing tips a little to adjust for this. There is a temptation to throw the plane upside down when it's finished, but it will fly much better if you launch it the way it looks like in the picture.

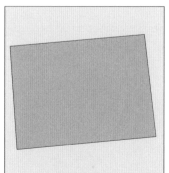

1. Start with a medium- to heavy-weight sheet of letter-size paper.

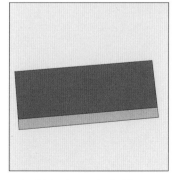

2. Fold it almost in half lengthwise. Leave about one finger width at the bottom edge of the paper.

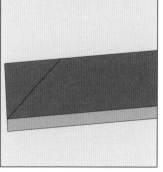

3. Fold the upper left corner down so the left edge of the paper lines up with the bottom edge of the top layer. Unfold after creasing.

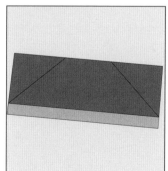

4. Repeat with the right corner. Crease, then unfold.

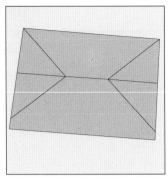

5. Unfold the paper and lay it flat on the work surface.

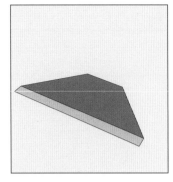

6. Grasp the ends of the horizontal crease and push them into the body, creating two triangular flaps inside. Press the fold flat.

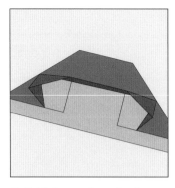

7. Fold the top layer back so the top edge lines up with the top fold. Bring the points at the left and right edges in toward each other, which will form two new creases.

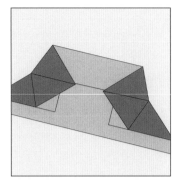

8. Be sure your plane matches the picture.

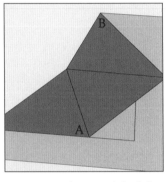

9. Here's a closeup of the left side, since the next fold is kind of tricky. Fold the bottom point A of the lower triangle up so it touches the top point B of the upper triangle.

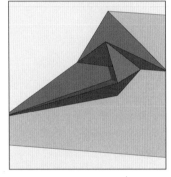

10. Make a fold along the existing crease between the two triangles.

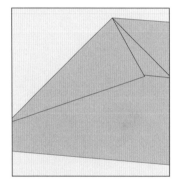

11. Two new creases are formed as you flatten the fold.

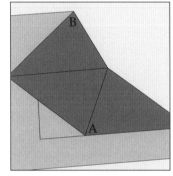

12. Now repeat the same steps on the right side of the craft. Again, a closeup provides a reference point.

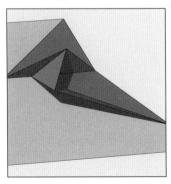

13. Make this fold precisely as you did on the left side.

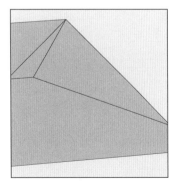

14. Flatten the fold, forming two new creases.

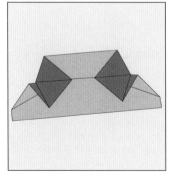

15. Fold down the upper left and right flaps, which were previously folded up.

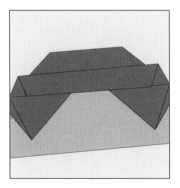

16. Fold the top layer on the nose down so the top edge lines up with the fold between the two triangles.

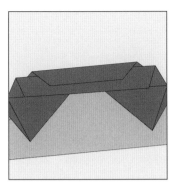

17. Fold the layer at the top of the nose over the fold just made. The edge comes over this fold about halfway.

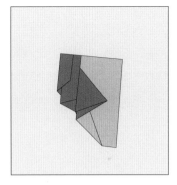

18. Flip over the paper so all the flaps are underneath and the long edge is to the right.

19. Fold the plane in half, bringing the top point down to the bottom.

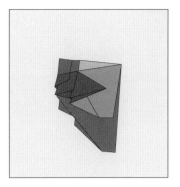

20. Crease the first wing flap up. The right point of the crease should be at the base of the body and the left point should be about halfway down the leftmost edge.

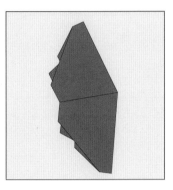

21. Flatten the fold.

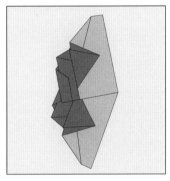

22. Flip over the plane so the first wing flap is underneath and the nose points left.

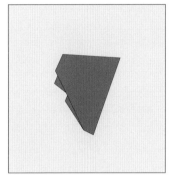

23. Crease down for the second wing flap. Be sure to line up the wing flaps for good balance.

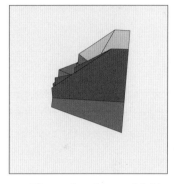

24. Flip up the plane and fold down the top wing flap. Make the left point of the crease less than halfway up from the body's bottom edge. The right edge should remain straight.

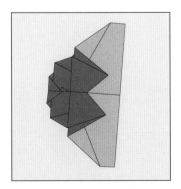

25. Flatten the fold.

26. Flip the plane over again so the first wing flap is underneath and the nose points to the left.

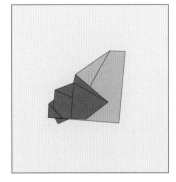

27. Make a crease for the second wing flap. Line up the wing flaps for good performance in flight. Open the wing flaps.

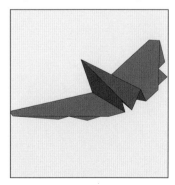

28. Set the wing angles equal, adjusting the dihedral angle so the wings are flat or slightly down—if the angle is up, the plane may fly wildly or even upside down.

VENUS

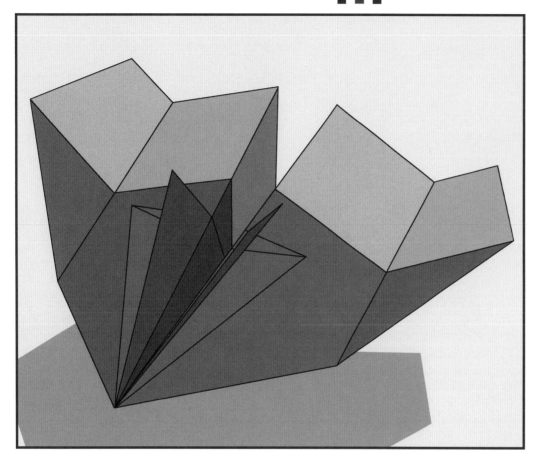

MODERATE

A craft with a menacing high-tech nose, this plane is a valuable addition to any fleet of starships. The four-pronged nose structure might cause you to question the plane's stability, but the extra weight allows the Venus to travel farther with a softer push, and the aesthetic properties are more than worth the precision that construction requires. Launch this craft gently at a slight upward angle. If the plane spirals or flutters to the ground, adjust the dihedral angle slightly upward so the wings are flatter. This craft is capable of long straight flights as long as it is launched correctly.

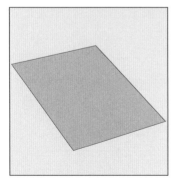

1. Start with a light- to medium-weight sheet of letter-size paper.

2. Fold the paper in half along its long edge. Make a sharp crease and unfold.

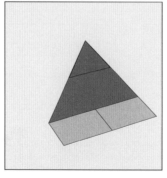

3. Fold down the upper left corner so the top edge lines up with the right side of the paper. Crease and unfold.

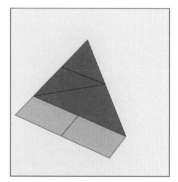

4. Repeat this fold with the upper right corner.

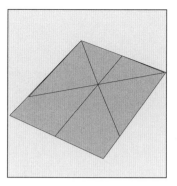

5. Lay the paper flat on the work surface.

6. Flip over the paper, keeping the diagonal creases toward the top.

7. Fold down the top edge so a new horizontal crease goes through the center point of the diagonal creases. Use a ruler to help align the fold.

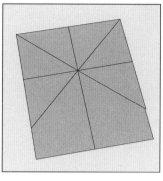

8. Flip over the paper, keeping the creases at the top.

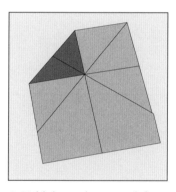

9. Fold down the upper left corner so the point touches the new horizontal crease.

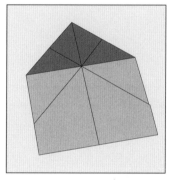

10. Fold down the upper right corner in the same manner, so it aligns with the new horizontal crease.

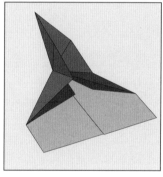

11. Grasp the ends of the horizontal crease and pull them in and down to meet at the center crease.

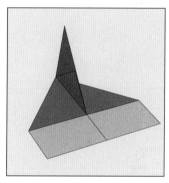

12. This causes a triangular flap to pop straight up.

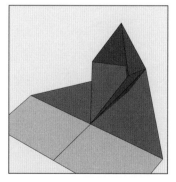

13. Pull the layers of the triangular flap apart along the diagonal creases. This will bring the top point down on the center crease.

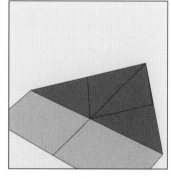

14. Flatten the fold, making sure your plane looks like the one in the picture.

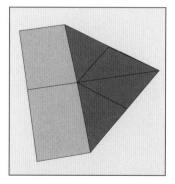

15. Rotate the paper so the nose is pointing right.

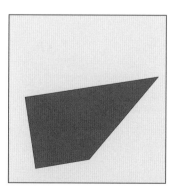

16. Fold the paper in half downward along the center crease. Line up the wing flaps so the plane will have good balance in flight.

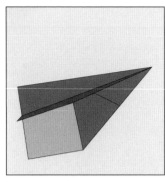

17. Make a crease for the first wing flap. The right point of the fold is at the tip of the nose and the left point is two finger widths down from the center fold.

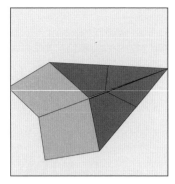

18. Flatten the fold. Press hard, since you're creasing through layers of paper.

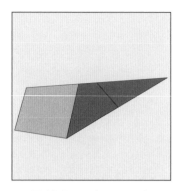

19. Flip over the plane so the first wing flap is underneath and the nose points right.

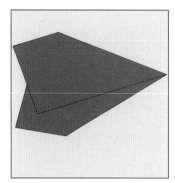

20. Fold down the second wing flap and crease. Line up the wing flaps for good flight performance. Be sure there are triangular nose flaps on either side of the plane's nose.

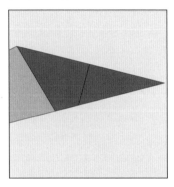

21. Flip up the plane, keeping the nose to the right.

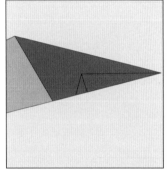

22. Fold down the nose flap so its top edge lines up with the bottom of the fuselage.

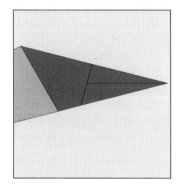

23. Unfold the flap.

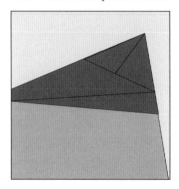

24. Rotate the paper so the nose is up and pointing away from you.

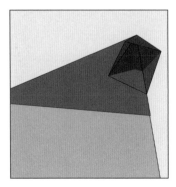

25. Pop open the nose flap. Press down on the top crease, and fold down the sides along the existing creases.

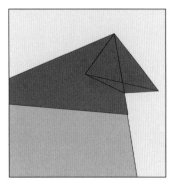

26. Press the fold flat against the work surface. Then orient your plane as shown in the next picutre.

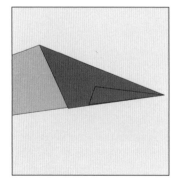

27. Fold the outer part of the nose flap up over the inner part along the crease at the base of the fuselage.

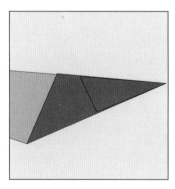

28. Flip over the plane, keeping the nose to the right and the wing flaps down.

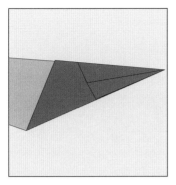

29. Fold the nose flap in half upward. Make a sharp crease and unfold the nose flap.

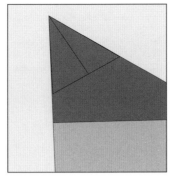

30. Rotate the plane so the nose points up.

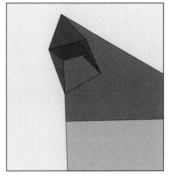

31. Pop open the nose flap. Press down on the top crease, folding the flaps along the existing creases.

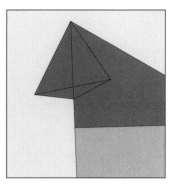

32. Press the fold flat against the work surface, creasing it hard. Turn the plane as shown in the next picture.

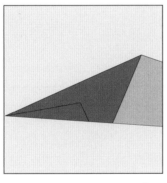

33. Fold the bottom part of the nose flap up along the base of the fuselage.

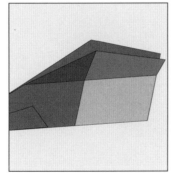

34. Fold down the top part of the wing flap. Make the crease parallel to the fuselage and three finger widths up from the bottom edge.

35. Flatten the fold.

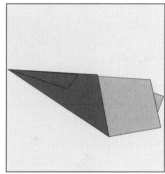

36. Flip over the plane, keeping the nose to the right.

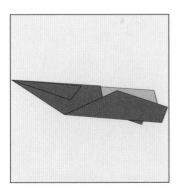

37. Fold up the other wing flap. Make sure the wings align for good balance.

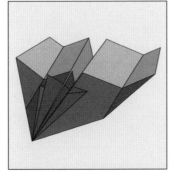

38. Open up the wing flaps so they're even. Open the four nose flaps so the angles between them are equal. The main wings should have a downward dihedral angle.

RULERS RULE

*F*olding the Venus will be made considerably easier if you crease the wing and nose folds against a metal ruler. The ruler will prevent the creases from going off line; in step 34 particularly, using a ruler will ensure that the first wing fold is parallel to the plane's fuselage—an essential ingredient in the successful flight of this plane. If the first wing is folded correctly, it's a simple matter to fold the second wing to match.

MERCURY

☰

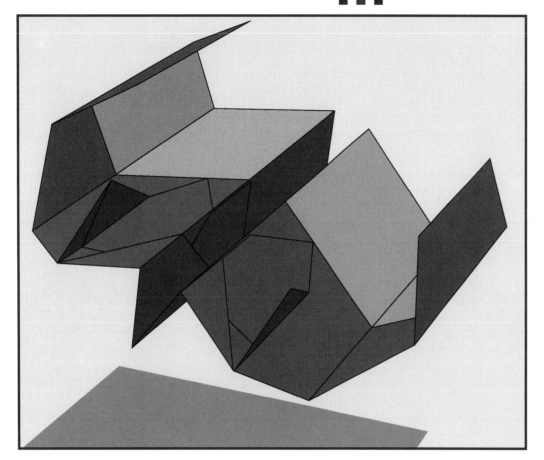

This compact little star-ship is a fun and versatile craft that can be trimmed for distance flying or for attacks. The flaps on the nose not only give the plane a snazzy high-tech appearance, they can also be adjusted to modify flight patterns in a subtle way. Launch the Mercury gently at a slight upward angle, or try throwing it straight up for long-distance glides. Play around with the dihedral angle and the angle of the wing flaps if the craft shows a tendency to turn over in flight.

1. Start this plane with a medium-weight sheet of letter-size paper.

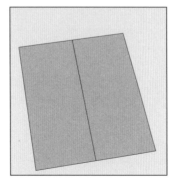

2. Fold the paper in half lengthwise. Make the crease sharp, then unfold.

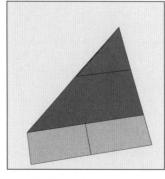

3. Fold down the upper left corner to touch the right edge of the paper, aligning the edges of the paper as you fold. Crease and unfold.

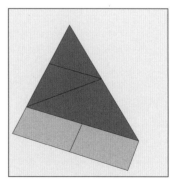

4. Repeat this fold with the upper right corner.

5. Flip over the paper, keeping the creases toward the top.

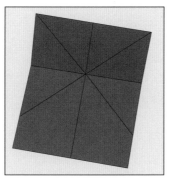

6. Fold down the top edge to make a new horizontal crease that runs through the intersection of the diagonal folds. Make the fold against a ruler to help align the crease.

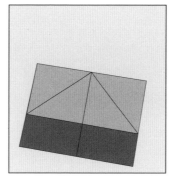

7. Flatten the crease.

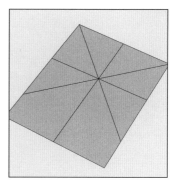

8. Unfold the crease and flip the paper over, keeping the new horizontal crease toward the top.

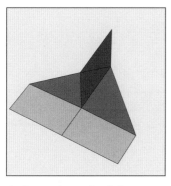

9. Grasp the ends of the new horizontal crease and pull them in and down toward the center crease. This will cause a vertical flap to pop up.

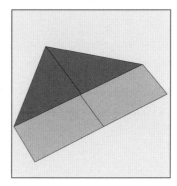

10. Pull the layers of the flap apart, bringing the free corners toward the edges of the paper along the diagonal creases. Press the fold flat.

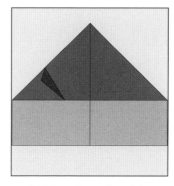

11. Fold up the point of the top left flap to touch the center crease.

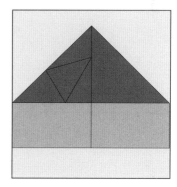

12. Flatten the fold.

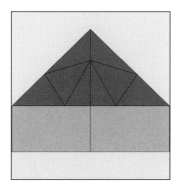

13. Repeat with the point of the top right flap, making sure that the points of both flaps meet.

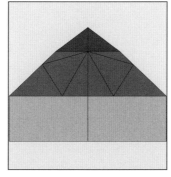

14. Fold down the tip of the nose to form a new horizontal crease just above the points of the flaps that you just folded.

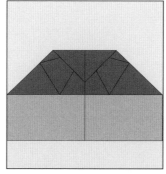

15. Make sure the tip of the nose covers the tips of the flaps underneath. Then flatten the fold.

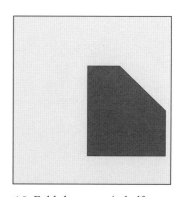

16. Fold the paper in half to the right along the center crease. Line up the wing flaps so the plane will have good balance. Make the crease as sharp as possible.

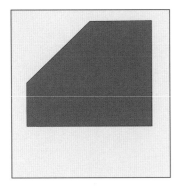

17. Rotate the plane so the nose is to the left and the wing flaps are up.

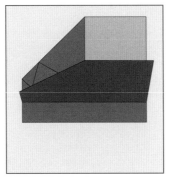

18. Fold down the first wing flap. The crease should be parallel to the fuselage and a little less than halfway up the edge of the nose.

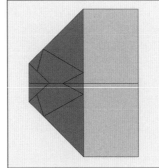

19. Be sure your plane matches the picture. Take a little time to make all the folds sharp.

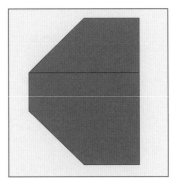

20. Flip over the plane so the first wing flap is underneath and the nose is pointing left.

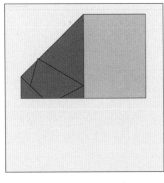

21. Fold up the second wing flap. It's important that both wings line up for good balance in flight.

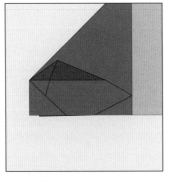

22. Fold down the point at the nose flap to create a small triangular flap. The crease should be parallel to the plane's fuselage.

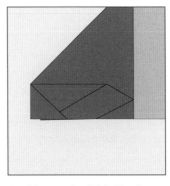

23. Flatten the fold. You have a lot of paper layers here, so press hard.

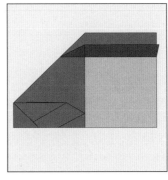

24. Fold down the top edge of the wing flap. The flap should be even with the fuselage and about two finger widths wide.

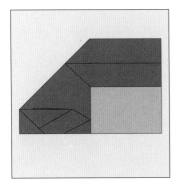

25. Make the fold sharp.

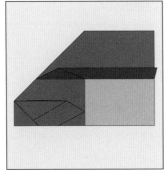

26. Fold the flap down on top of itself, keeping the new crease parallel to the fuselage.

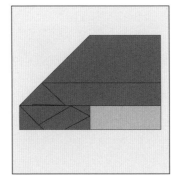

27. Check to make sure your plane matches the picture. Adjust the flap you just folded if it doesn't. When things are right, flatten the fold.

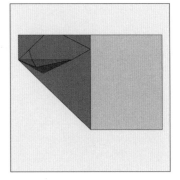

28. Flip over the plane, keeping the nose to the left. Fold up the point at the nose flap to create a new triangular flap. Make sure the crease is parallel to the fuselage.

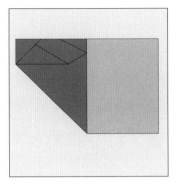

29. Make the fold sharp.

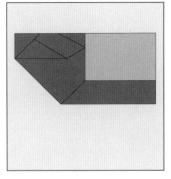

30. Fold up the bottom edge of the wing flap. The flap should be parallel to the fuselage and about two finger widths wide.

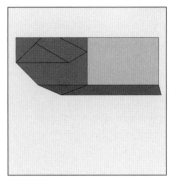

31. Flatten the fold.

32. Fold up the flap on top of itself, keeping the crease parallel to the edge of the plane's fuselage.

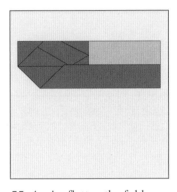

33. Again, flatten the fold, then turn your plane so that the nose is facing you. Turn the plane upside down so the little wings are on top.

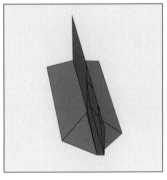

34. Open up the first two layers of the outer wing flaps, making their angles equal. Then open all the wing flaps.

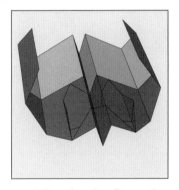

35. Adjust the wing-flap angles so they're symmetrical. Make the nose flaps stick straight up from the plane. Adjust the main wing flaps at a downward dihedral angle.

FINGER-WIDTH MEASUREMENT

*T*his craft calls for using the width of your index finger as a measuring tool. While not particularly precise, finger-width measurement will at least get your creases in the ball park. In the Mercury, however, the folds where finger-width measurement is required are somewhat critical—since the width of fingers differ, you may need to fudge the measurements in steps 24 and 30 to get the folds on your plane to match the pictures in steps 27 and 33. Don't be afraid to tweak the measurements if it results in more successful flight.

TYPHOON

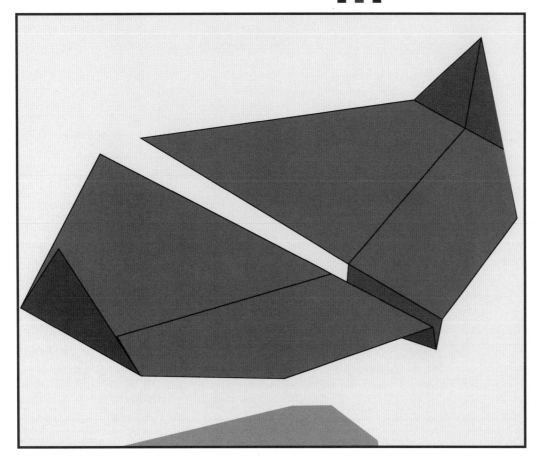

MODERATE

This wing-type craft has an extremely small fuse-lage and large broad wings for sweeping glider-style flights. It is moderately dif-ficult to make because of the number of folds required and the need to make sharp creases through several lay-ers of paper. When launch-ing the Typhoon, give the craft a gentle push at a slight upward angle. A hard throw can cause looping. If the plane tends to circle back, adjust the wing-tip flaps until they are vertical. When well trimmed, this plane will fly in a straight path for a long time.

1. Start with a letter-size sheet of medium- to heavy-weight paper. Orient the paper horizontally.

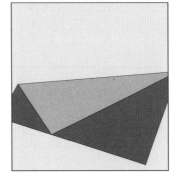

2. Fold down the upper left corner so it touches the bottom edge of the sheet and make a sharp crease.

3. The crease must split the upper right corner of the paper exactly, which can be tricky to get just right. Unfold the paper.

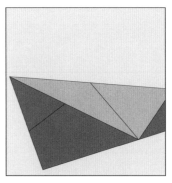

4. Repeat the fold on the opposite side, taking care to crease the paper exactly through the point of the upper left corner.

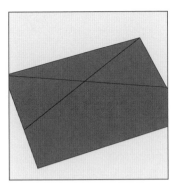

5. After making the second crease, unfold the paper so it's completely flat.

6. Reposition the sheet and fold it exactly in half, bringing the short edges together. Crease, then unfold.

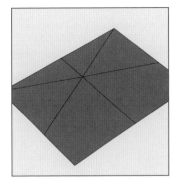

7. Rotate the sheet to prepare for reversing the upper section of the two creases you just made.

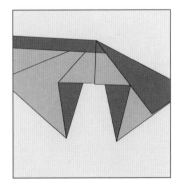

8. "Reversing" simply means that you fold a crease the opposite way. Reverse both creases from the upper corners to the center line.

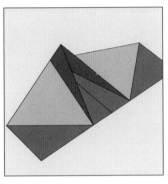

9. Gently pull the upper corners of the paper together to create upright flaps.

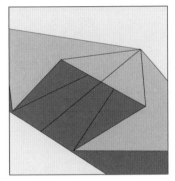

10. Flatten the upright flaps, aligning the center creases. In so doing, you'll create two new creases. Push them down flat, making sure they're even.

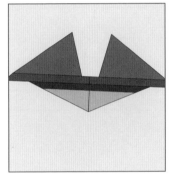

11. Turn over the sheet so the point is down. Bring the top edge down, creasing all the way across the sheet.

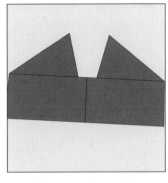

12. When creasing, make sure that the ends of the crease touch the points where the diagonal folds end on the layer beneath.

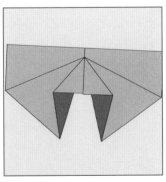

13. Turn the plane over so the two tails point down.

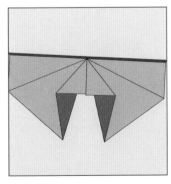

14. Fold down the top edge to make a flap. The flap should slightly overlap the point.

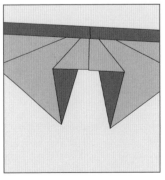

15. Run the flap all the way across the top edge of the paper, keeping the crease parallel to the edge.

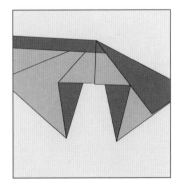

16. Crease a new flap that extends from the top of the plane's center line to the bottom edge of the diagonal flap below.

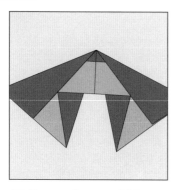

17. Repeat the same fold on the opposite side of the plane.

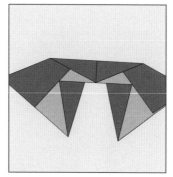

18. Bring down the point so it touches the center line and make a sharp crease.

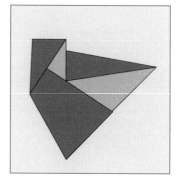

19. Turn over the plane and rotate it so the flat nose points left and the two triangular tails point right.

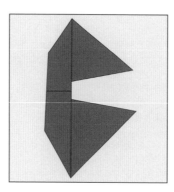

20. Fold down the plane in half exactly along the existing center crease.

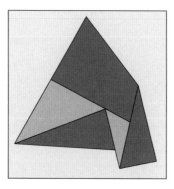

21. Rotate the plane so that the flat nose is toward the right and the pointed tail is toward the left.

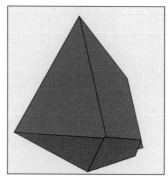

22. Fold down the top wing through the point of the nose. This section is quite thick, so you need to press hard.

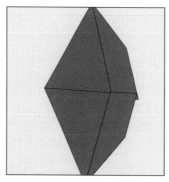

23. When you look at the folded plane from the top, the wings should meet without a space in between.

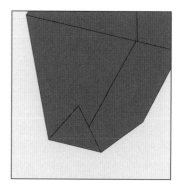

24. Fold up a small flap about two finger widths from the wing tip. Make sure to keep this new crease parallel to the main wing crease.

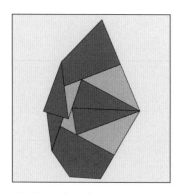

25. Turn the plane end over end, keeping the wing-tip flap facing you.

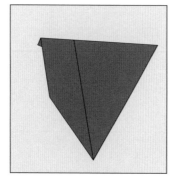

26. Fold the second wing as you did the first, bringing it through the tip of the nose. Adjust the wings so they're the same on both sides.

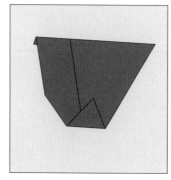

27. Fold up the wing tip, matching the new wing tip to the existing one. Open the wings and wing tips.

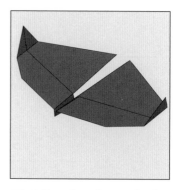

28. Adjust the wings so both sides match. Set the dihedral angle slightly upward—it will relax during flight to become nearly flat.

HURRICANE

EASY

This flying-wing-style plane is fairly easy to construct, once you get the hang of the origami-type folds sometimes called "fortune-telling" folds. Make the craft from medium- to heavy-weight letter paper. When properly folded, the Hurricane flies an extremely straight path and is capable of astonishing maneuvers, depending on how hard it is thrown. Launch the plane gently for long straight glides. Throw it hard at a sideways angle if you want to play with looping and acrobatic actions.

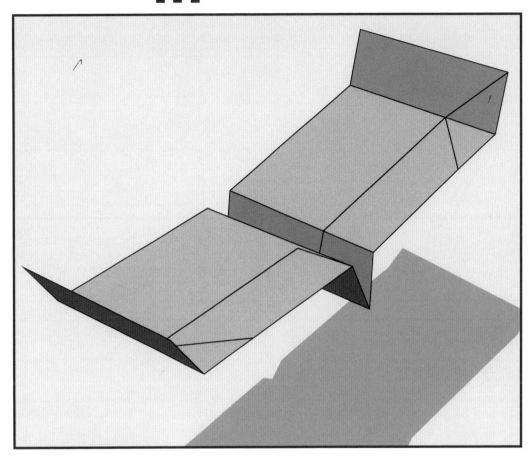

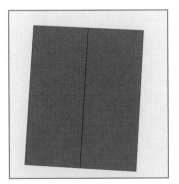

1. Fold a letter-size sheet of paper in half lengthwise and crease sharply. Then unfold the paper.

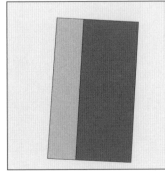

2. Fold in the left edge of the sheet to the center crease.

3. Make another crease by folding the right edge of the top flap back to meet the left edge of the flap

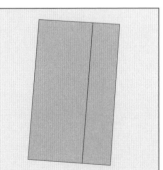

4. Turn the sheet over and position it so all the folds you made are on the right.

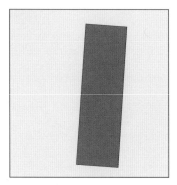

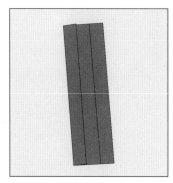

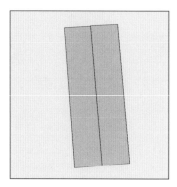

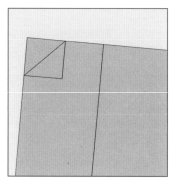

5. Fold the left edge of the paper over to the right edge and crease hard.

6. Turn over the sheet from right to left. The layered flaps should be along the left edge.

7. Grasp the top two layers of paper and open to the right along the original center crease. Keeping the same surface up, turn the sheet so the flap faces left.

8. Grasp the top two layers of paper at the upper left corner. Pull down to form a flap. The edges of the flap must be at a right angle to the paper edges.

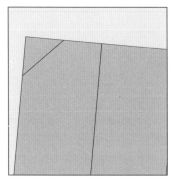

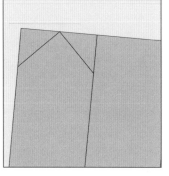

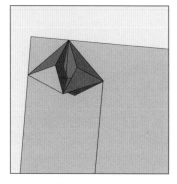

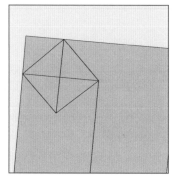

9. Unfold the flap and make a mirror image on the other side of the flap.

10. To make the mirror-image fold, simply turn down the opposite corner. Crease sharply, then unfold.

11. Refold the triangles, then fold both triangles backward at the base to make a new crease. Open the triangles to form a new fold by pulling down at the point.

12. Press the layers flat. Keeping the same surface up, turn the sheet end for end. The layered flaps will now be along the right edge.

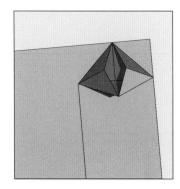

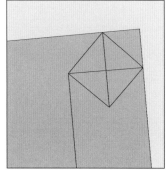

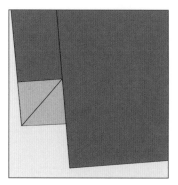

13. Repeat the same steps on the upper right end of the paper. Keep your creases sharp and the paper edges aligned as closely as you can.

14. After opening the triangle to create the new fold, firmly press down the flap as before.

15. Turn over the paper so the flaps are on the left side.

16. Make a tab by folding up all the layers on the bottom left edge.

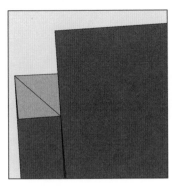

17. Create another tab at the top of the paper.

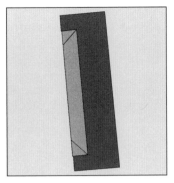

18. Fold over the flap containing the tabs to the right. Crease sharply.

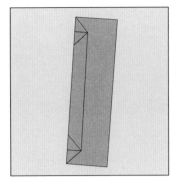

19. Turn over the paper end for end, keeping the flaps on the left.

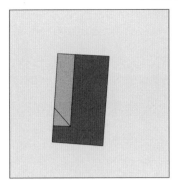

20. Fold the craft in half by bringing the top edge to the bottom. Line up all the edges and make a nice sharp crease.

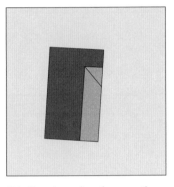

21. Reorient the plane so the newest crease is along the bottom edge. The edge with the flaps is to the right.

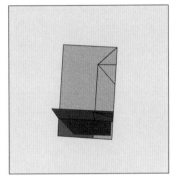

22. Crease down the first wing fold, measuring up two finger widths from the bottom. The crease must be parallel to the bottom edge.

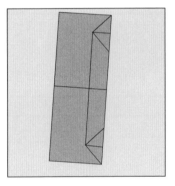

23. Open the plane completely and press flat on the work surface.

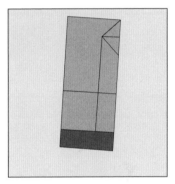

24. Fold up the bottom edge, running the fold through the existing crease in the triangular flap.

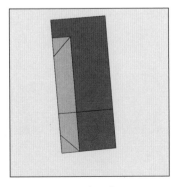

25. Turn over the plane, maintaining the orientation of the top and bottom, so the flaps are on the left side.

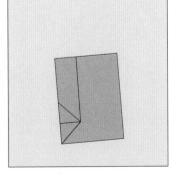

26. Fold the top edge toward the inside to make the second wing crease. It must match the one below. Line up all the edges and crease sharply.

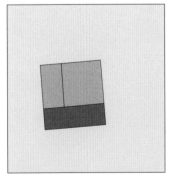

27. Fold up the bottom edge to make the crease that forms the second wing. Open the plane and adjust all the angles so both sides are identical.

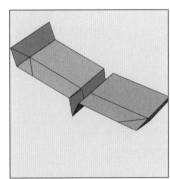

28. The dihedral angle of the wings should be flat to slightly downward. Lastly, adjust the vertical stabilizers so they're straight and even.

TORNADO

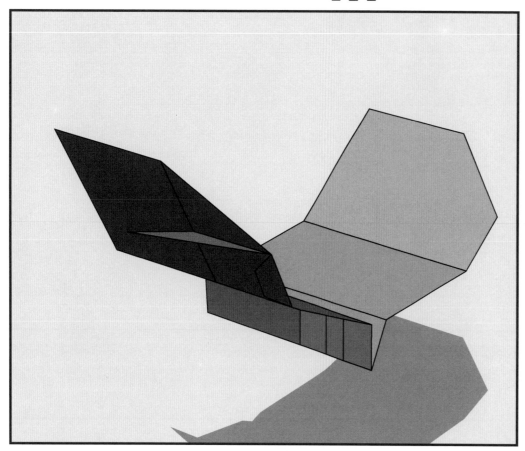

This versatile craft is a robust flyer. Good in all types of wind conditions, the Tornado can be trimmed and flown in a variety of different configurations. It's moderately easy to build and once you're finished, you can experiment with the wing sections and triangular flaps to produce different flight patterns. By setting the dihedral angle downward and the triangular flaps perfectly vertical, for example, you can achieve impressively long, straight flights. Launch this plane with a moderate to hard throw. Light throws will make the plane glide while hard throws will result in acrobatics.

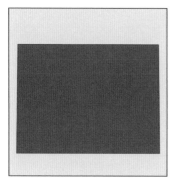

1. Start with a letter-size sheet of medium- to light-weight paper.

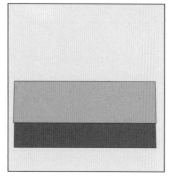

2. Fold down the paper along the top edge to about two or three finger widths from the bottom. If the flap is either too long or too short, the plane won't fly well.

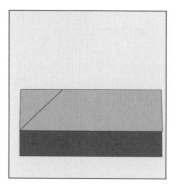

3. Crease the upper left corner by folding it down. The left edge of the fold should fall along the edge of the top flap.

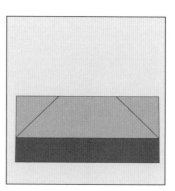

4. Repeat the same fold on the right corner.

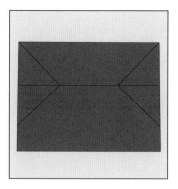

5. Unfold the paper. The next step is to use the diagonal creases on each side of the paper to pull in the edges where they meet the crease.

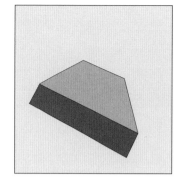

6. To do this, bring down the top edge along the first crease so it's back where it was after the first fold.

7. Now fold the creases into the plane, and turn the paper so the folds point up.

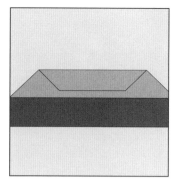

8. Make a new crease by bringing the top edge down, but miss the edge of the top layer by about one finger width. The crease must be parallel to the bottom edge.

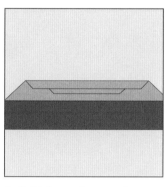

9. Fold down the top edge again, leaving a finger width between the fold and the edge of the previous flap. Make the crease parallel to the bottom edge. Flatten the folds.

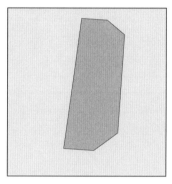

10. Flip over the paper and turn it so that the flaps you just folded face right.

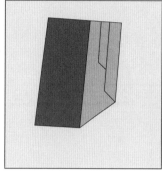

11. Fold the top edge down to meet the bottom edge.

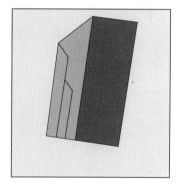

12. Reposition the plane so that the new crease is toward the bottom and the folds face to the left.

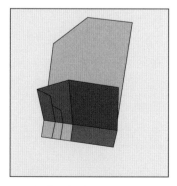

13. Make the first wing crease by folding down the top layer. The new crease should be about a large finger width above the bottom edge and parallel to it.

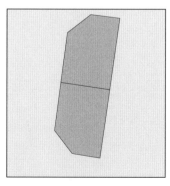

14. Press the plane flat.

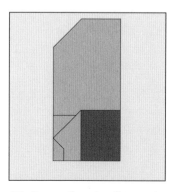

15. Crease the wing flap again by folding the bottom edge to the middle. Flap size isn't critical, but the crease should be parallel to the others and the edges should line up.

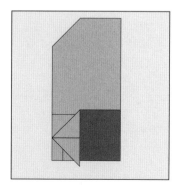

16. Fold down the top triangular layer to form a flap that points downward. Make sure the new crease is parallel to the bottom edge.

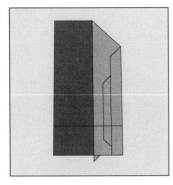

17. Turn the plane over from left to right, keeping the triangular flap pointed down. You will now duplicate the wing-flap folds on the other side of the plane.

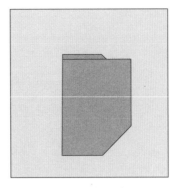

18. Fold down the other wing, creating a crease that matches the one below it.

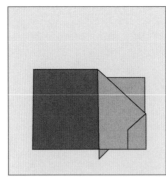

19. Fold up the bottom edge of the wing you just folded down so it matches the flap created on the opposite wing. Match all the edges and the creases, too.

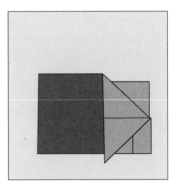

20. Bring down the top layer of the triangle to form a flap that points downward. Try to match the flap beneath it, which was created on the other wing.

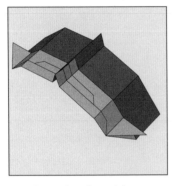

21. Open the plane (shown upside down for clarity), adust all the angles to be the same, and open and adjust the small triangular flaps. Set the dihedral flat or a bit up.

REVERSING THE CREASE

*W*ith certain folds, it's easier to create a sharp crease if you pinch the crease in the opposite direction before making the new fold. This is called "reversing the crease," and it simply means that you use existing creases—just inside out. Step 6 of the Tornado involves the reversing of creases. When properly constructed, you'll find the Tornado to be the most versatile of the flying wings, performing well in all wind conditions whether trimmed for distance or loops.

CHINOOK

MODERATE

This plane is moderately easy to fold using light- to medium-weight paper. The hardest part of construction is forming the vertical stabilizer fins, which are folded the same way four separate times. These fins at the ends of the wings lead to extremely straight flight paths. For the best performance, launch the Chinook from a high place with a gentle throw. This craft will fly straight with a slight bouncing motion when folded correctly.

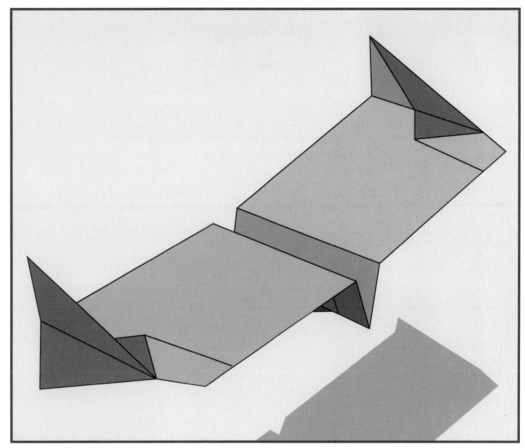

1. Start with a letter-size sheet and fold it in half by bringing the two long edges together. Crease and unfold.

2. Bring the top edge down and the bottom edge up to meet the center crease. Flatten and unfold.

3. Fold the paper down along the center crease. Position the paper so the center crease is farthest away from you.

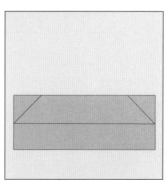

4. Fold the upper left and right corners to meet the crease in the middle of the body. Crease the paper hard and unfold.

5. Open up the sheet completely. Prepare to reverse the direction of some of the creases to tuck the triangular portions into the body.

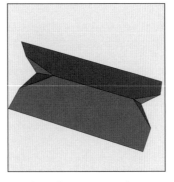

6. Close the paper on the center crease again, but bring the triangular creases in to form two triangular flaps inside the body of the plane.

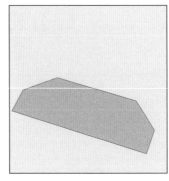

7. Flatten the folds.

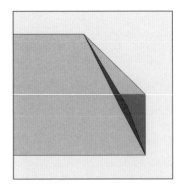

8. Grasp the point at the right end of the center crease and fold it down. The crease should run from the lower right corner of the paper to the top edge.

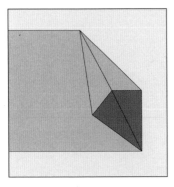

9. Flatten the fold completely, making sure your plane looks like the picture.

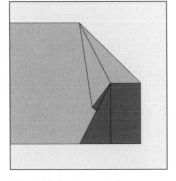

10. Fold the lower right corner of the top flap to the left. The crease should be vertical, with the bottom edge of the flap running along the bottom edge of the paper.

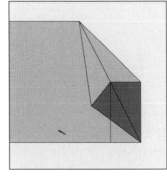

11. Unfold the flap that you just created.

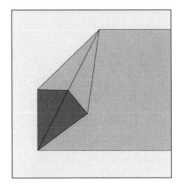

12. Repeat the fold on the left side, pulling the point at the left end of the center crease down so the crease runs from the lower left to the upper left corners of the paper.

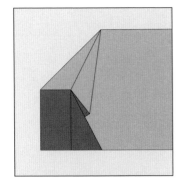

13. Fold the lower left corner of the top flap to the right, making a vertical crease, as before. Make sure the bottom edge of the flap meets the bottom edge of the paper.

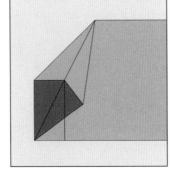

14. Unfold the crease and press it completely flat on the work surface.

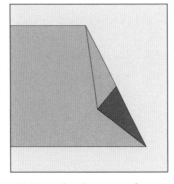

15. Turn the sheet over from right to left and position it with the center crease away from you. Make a fold on the right side identical to the one behind the body.

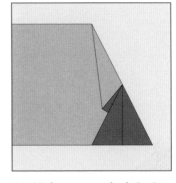

16. Make a crease by bringing the lower right corner of the top flap to the left. As before, the crease is vertical. Its bottom edge runs along the paper's bottom edge.

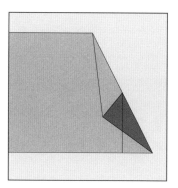

17. Unfold the crease.

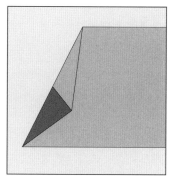

18. Make a fold on the left side identical to the fold behind the body.

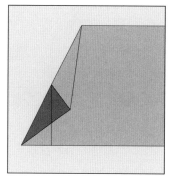

19. Make a vertical crease just as you did on the right side, and unfold.

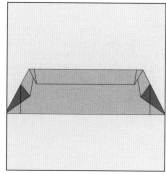

20. Fold down the top fold to create a new flap. The top edge should line up with the horizontal crease (not shown in the picture).

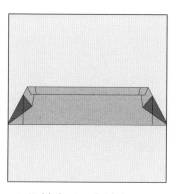

21. Fold the top fold down again in half to the fold just created. Crease sharply—the multiple layers of paper will make this a bit difficult.

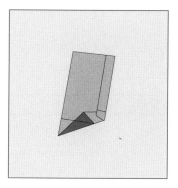

22. Turn over the paper so the flap is underneath and the top is facing right. Fold the top wing down in half to meet the bottom as shown here.

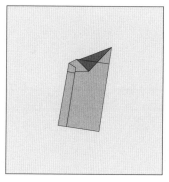

23. Rotate the plane so the crease that was just formed is facing toward you.

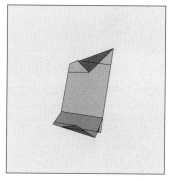

24. Form the wing by folding down the top flap. Make the crease about two finger widths above the previous crease and parallel to it.

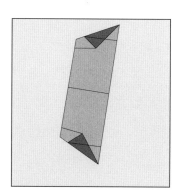

25. Flatten the fold.

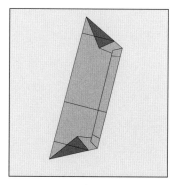

26. Turn the plane over from right to left, keeping the wing just formed toward you.

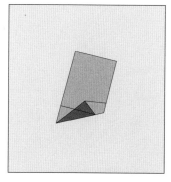

27. To form the second wing, bring the other flap down, making a crease identical to the previous one. Line up all the edges before creasing.

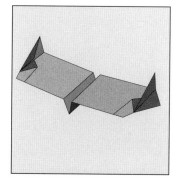

28. Open the plane and make the angles equal on both sides. The dihedral angle should be flat or slightly upward. Open the wing flaps and set them so they're vertical.

MONSOON

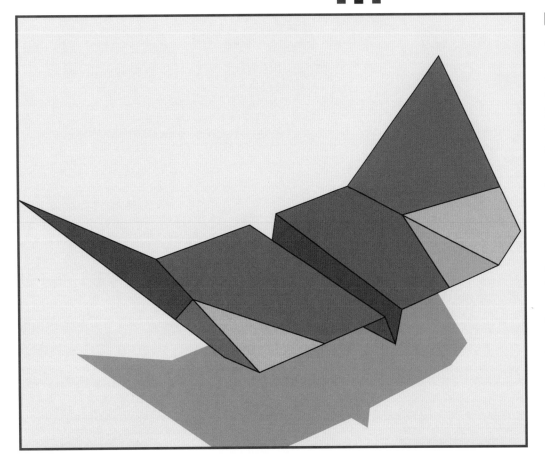

MODERATE

The elegant wing design of the Monsoon combines outstanding elements of the flying-wing style to produce the best all-around craft in this category. This plane works best with light-to medium-weight letter-size paper. Launch the Monsoon with a moderate to hard throw. It will fly well in most conditions, and can be thrown hard at a high angle for long soaring flights. Angling the dihedral angle downward and the wing flaps upward gives the craft stability and helps straighten out the flight path.

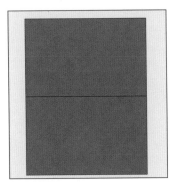

1. Fold a letter-size sheet in half by bringing the short edges together. Unfold after creasing hard.

2. Bring the top edge down to meet the crease just formed. Crease, flatten, and unfold.

3. Repeat the fold using the bottom edge of the paper. Then turn the sheet so the creases are vertical.

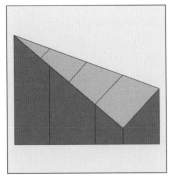

4. Bring down the upper right corner of the sheet to touch the right-most vertical crease. Run the left end of the new crease through the upper left corner. Repeat the fold on the left side of the paper.

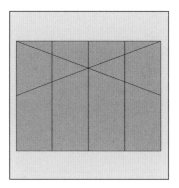

5. Unfold the sheet and turn it over from left to right. The diagonal creases should be toward the top.

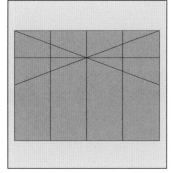

6. Bring down the top edge of the paper to make a new crease that goes through the intersection of the two diagonal creases. Unfold.

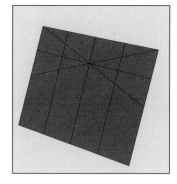

7. Turn over the sheet from left to right.

8. Fold down the top flap, bringing in the ends of the horizontal crease. All the creases should be going in the proper direction, so the flaps will come in naturally.

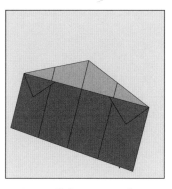

9. Press all the creases down flat and be sure your plane matches the picture.

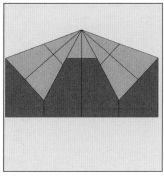

10. Bring down the left and right flaps on the top layer to form two large triangles. Press down to create new creases in line with the inner edges of the flaps in step 9.

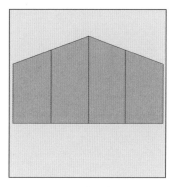

11. Turn over the sheet, keeping the point facing up.

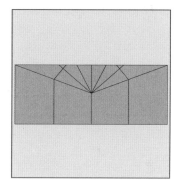

12. Bring the pointed tip down, forming a new horizontal crease. The crease should end at the base of the triangle. Make the crease as sharp as possible through all the layers.

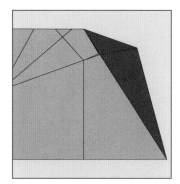

13. Bring down the upper right corner to form a crease that touches the lower right corner. The left end of this crease should touch the vertical crease created during steps 2 and 3.

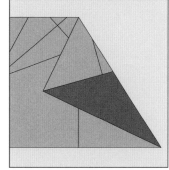

14. Flatten the fold.

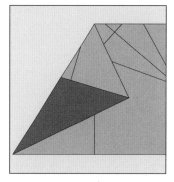

15. Repeat this fold on the left side.

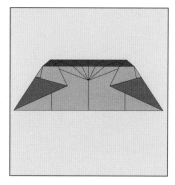

16. Fold the top edge downward to form a new flap. This flap should just cover the downward pointed flap beneath it and should be parallel to the bottom edge.

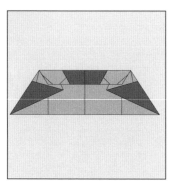
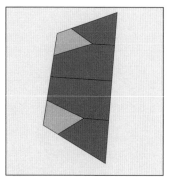
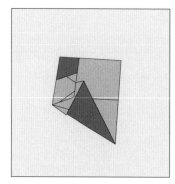
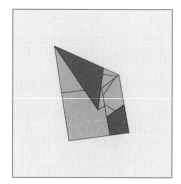

17. There are many layers, so press hard and make the crease as sharp as possible.

18. Turn over the plane and position it so the side with all the flaps faces left.

19. Fold the plane in half downward along the center crease. Make sure all the edges line up.

20. Rotate the plane so that the center crease is toward you and the wing tips are pointing away.

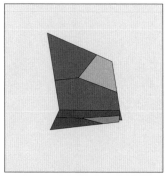
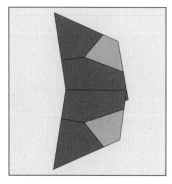
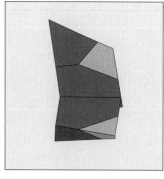
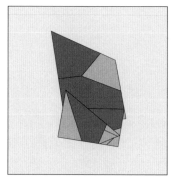

21. Bring down the top layer to form the first main wing crease. The right end of this crease is a finger width above the center crease, and the left end is two finger widths above.

22. Flatten the fold.

23. Fold the wing tip up along the crease on the back of the wing. Be sure to fold the tip up so it will look like step 24, not down, as it may look like in this picture.

24. Crease all the layers of paper as sharply as possible.

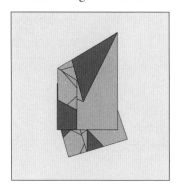
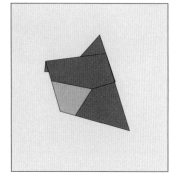

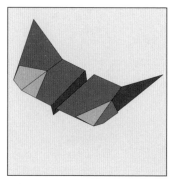

25. Turn the plane over from left to right, keeping the wing tip pointed away from you.

26. Bring down the other wing to make a crease that matches the one beneath it. Line up all the edges before flattening this crease.

27. Fold up the wing tip along the crease on the back of the wing. Press hard.

28. Open the plane and adjust the angles to be the same on both sides. The dihedral angle should be flat to slightly downward. Angle the wing tips upward.

SALMON

EASY

*T*his delta-wing-style flyer requires a few odd diagonal folds, yet the plane is extremely symmetrical in design. The production is easy as long as you are sure to make the diagonal folds precisely and crease them sharply. Launch the Salmon with a gentle throw at a slight upward angle. A hard throw will cause the plane to lose its shape and flutter to the ground. This craft will open up a little bit as it flies but that is normal. The Salmon will float and fly well from a high place when trimmed properly. Keep an eye on the tail flaps, which should remain as vertical as possible.

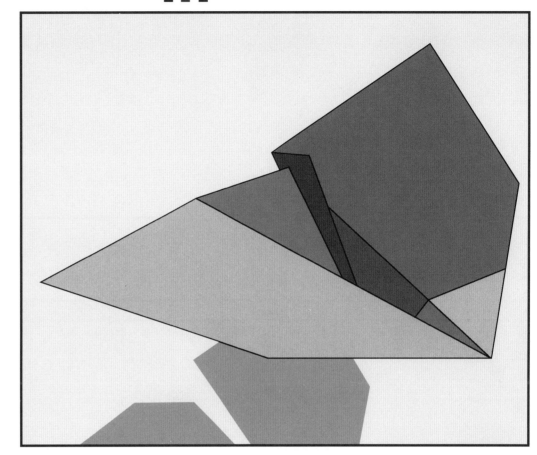

1. This plane requires a sheet of medium- to heavy-weight letter paper cut in half the long way.

2. Fold the paper in half from top to bottom.

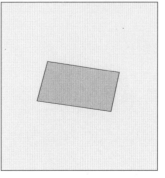

3. Then fold the paper in half once again.

4. Unfold the creases so the paper is flat on the work surface.

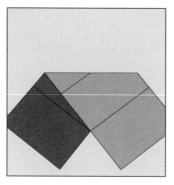

5. Fold down the point at the left end of the crease that's first from the top. It should touch the point at the right end of the crease that's first from the bottom.

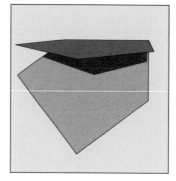

6. Flip the paper over and turn it so the crease you just made is on the right.

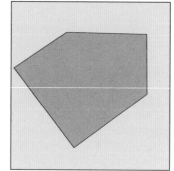

7. Fold the paper in half.

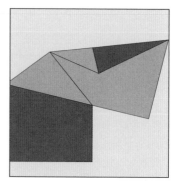

8. As you make this fold, carefully match up the top and bottom points.

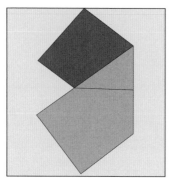

9. Unfold the crease.

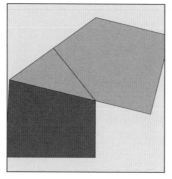

10. Flip over the paper and rotate it so the fold faces left.

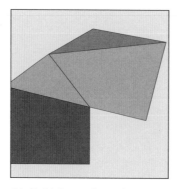

11. Fold down the point at the top of the paper.

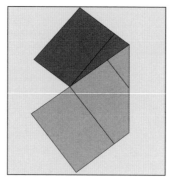

12. Run the crease between the upper right corner of the paper and the top of the first diagonal crease.

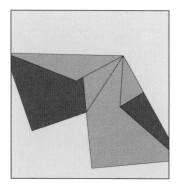

13. Repeat the fold on the left side of the plane, taking care to match the new triangular flap to the one you just made.

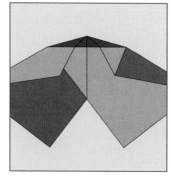

14. Fold the tip of the nose down so the top point hits the center crease.

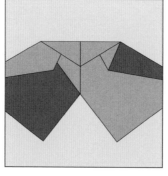

15. Use the diagonal point on the right flap as a reference for making the nose crease, as shown here.

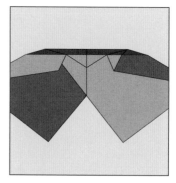

16. Fold down the top of the nose so the tip is underneath.

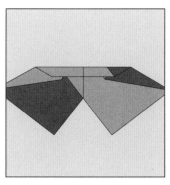

17. The crease line must be parallel to the top edge. When you've got it right, press down hard on the crease.

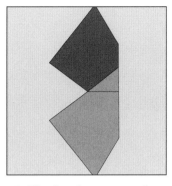

18. Flip the plane over and turn it so the nose points to the right.

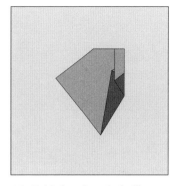

19. Fold the plane in half from top to bottom along the center line crease. Align the two halves for good balance.

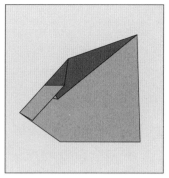

20. Turn the plane so the nose points to the left.

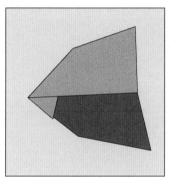

21. Fold down the first wing flap. Crease the paper from the tip of the nose to about two finger widths up from the bottom edge of the fuselage on the right.

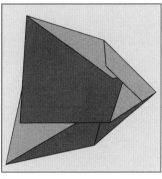

22. Flip over the plane so the nose points to the right.

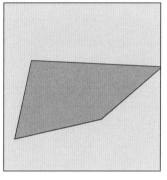

23. Fold down the second wing flap. Line up the flaps for good balance.

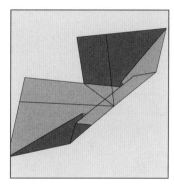

24. Open up the wing flaps so that the plane is flat on the work surface.

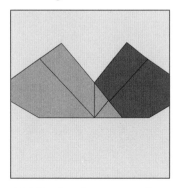

25. Flip the plane over and rotate it so the nose points down. Fold down a crease on the right side of the tail.

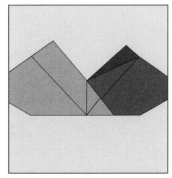

26. Begin the crease on the left at the point where the tail flaps come together. End the crease at the upper right diagonal crease on the flap.

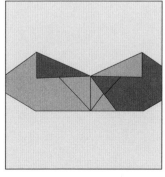

27. Fold down the crease on the left side of the tail in the same way. Close the wing flaps and extend the tail flaps as you bring the fuselage halves together.

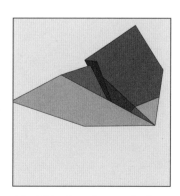

28. Align the wings and trim the tail flaps so they're even. The dihedral angle should be flat or slightly down; the tail flaps must be vertical.

MINNOW
III

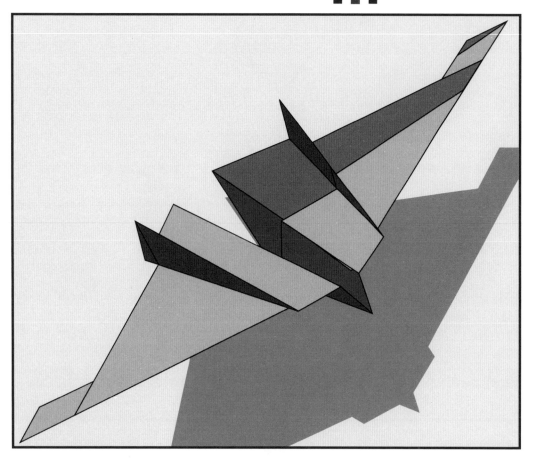

MODERATE

This broad-winged craft uses the paper's maximum length along the diagonal for its wingspan. It's moderately difficult to fold, but worth making, because it can be thrown aggressively for an impressive flight when properly trimmed. Launch with a moderate to hard throw at a slightly upward angle. If needed for stability, you can hold the sides of the craft together with a small piece of tape to maintain an upward dihedral angle. Should the plane roll to the right or left, you can adjust the opposite wing tip to compensate.

1. Start with a sheet of letter-size paper that's of light to medium weight.

2. Fold the paper in half, running the crease from the upper right-hand corner to the lower-left corner.

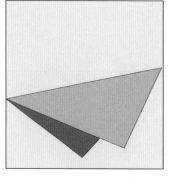

3. This is a long crease and can be a bit tricky, so take your time.

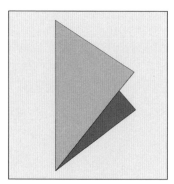

4. Turn the paper so the crease is on the left.

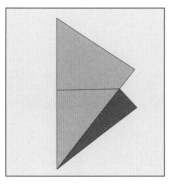

5. Fold the paper in half from the top to the bottom. Unfold after creasing.

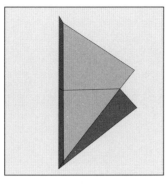

6. Fold over the left edge of the paper, making its width about the size of a finger.

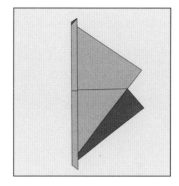

7. Take care that the crease is straight with its top edge and parallel to its bottom edge.

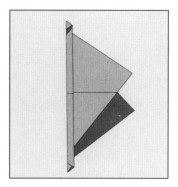

8. Again, fold the left edge of the paper over on itself. The top of the crease must be parallel to the bottom of the paper. Make this crease as sharp as possible.

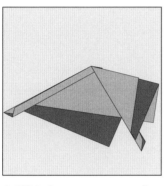

9. With the center crease of the folded edge between your left thumb and index fingers, flip down the upper flap so the folded edge aligns with the center crease.

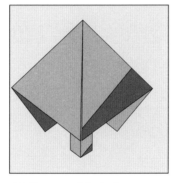

10. Repeat with the bottom flap. Press the crease hard.

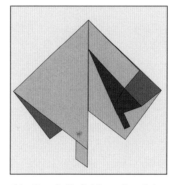

11. Carefully fold up the right top-most flap.

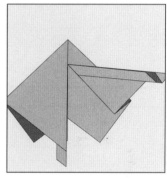

12. Make the crease about the width of two fingers down from the tip of the nose. Keep the crease parallel to the bottom edge.

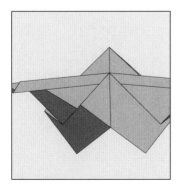

13. Repeat the fold on the left, using the same reference point of two fingers down from the nose tip. Carefully line up the left and right sides for good balance.

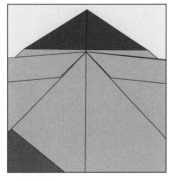

14. Fold down the tip of the nose so that it touches the center crease.

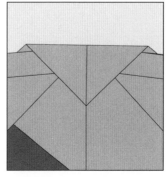

15. Make the new crease as close as possible to the wing flaps. Press down hard to flatten the crease.

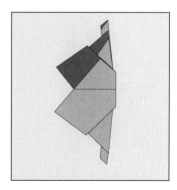

16. Flip over the plane and rotate it so the nose points to the right.

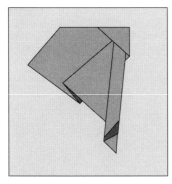

17. Fold down the plane in half along the center crease, lining up the sides for good balance. The paper in the nose section is so thick that it may split; this is normal.

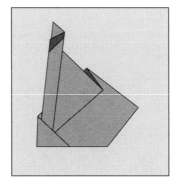

18. Rotate the plane so the nose points left and the wing flaps are up.

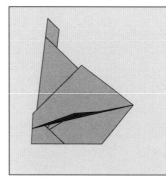

19. Make a crease for the first wing flap.

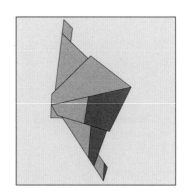

20. Use the right-most point of the fuselage as a reference point for creasing. The left point should be about one finger width up from the bottom edge of the fuselage.

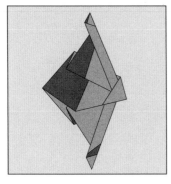

21. Flip over the plane and rotate it so the first wing flap is underneath and the nose points to the right.

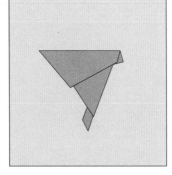

22. Crease the second wing flap by folding down the top flap. Line up the wing flaps for good balance and flying performance.

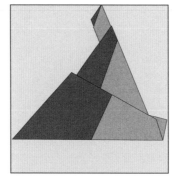

23. Flip over the plane so the wing flaps are up and the nose still points to the right.

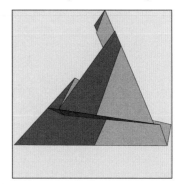

24. Make a crease for the first winglet by carefully folding down the flap.

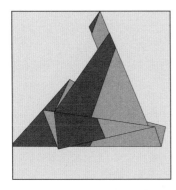

25. Run the crease from the upper right point of the top-most flap to the point where the top layer of paper joins the layer underneath.

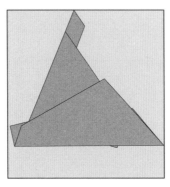

26. Turn the plane so the first winglet is underneath and the nose points left.

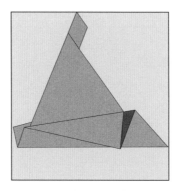

27. Crease the second winglet in the same manner as the one just created. Open the wing flaps and the winglets and adjust so they're even.

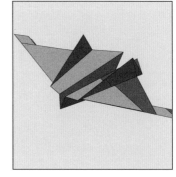

28. Balance the left and right sides for success in flight. Set the dihedral slightly upward and curl up the wing tips slightly. Position the winglets as close to vertical as possible.

TROUT

MODERATE

The odd diagonal folds in this delta-wing-style craft work best with light- to medium-weight paper. This plane is somewhat challenging to construct in that it's sensitive to uneven folding and the setting of the dihedral angle—the dihedral angle should be set somewhat down with the outer wing flaps upward at a corresponding angle. Launch the Trout with either a moderate or hard level throw or at a slight downward angle. Some up elevator may have to be added to the tail flaps. Depending on how you trim this craft, it will either glide smoothly or soar at high speed through acrobatic flights—experiment!

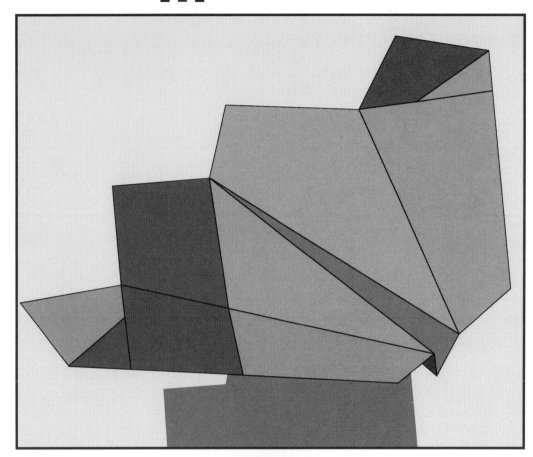

1. Fold a letter-size sheet of paper exactly in half. Unfold after creasing.

2. Crease the paper in half the other way and unfold. Turn the paper as shown in the next picture.

3. Grasp the right end of the short center crease and pull it down. The object is to partially cover the bottom part of the long center crease.

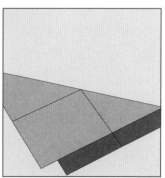

4. You'll be left with a protruding strip of paper about two fingers wide at the bottom. When creasing the fold, make sure the edge of the fold is parallel to the bottom edge of the paper.

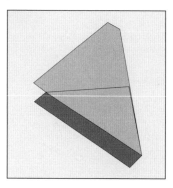

5. Turn the paper so the new crease is on the right. Fold the paper in half, bringing the top point down. Unfold the paper after creasing.

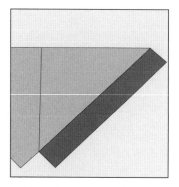

6. Turn the paper so the folded edge is at the top. The next fold is tricky, and involves the protruding strip you created in step 4.

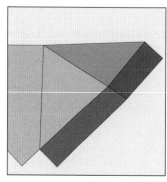

7. The fold starts at the top of the center crease. You swing down a flap, making the top point of the protruding strip touch the bottom edge of the strip, as shown next.

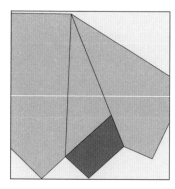

8. Note the relationship of the top point of the protruding strip to the bottom paper edge. When you've got it right, make the crease and unfold the paper.

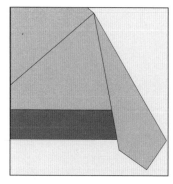

9. Fold over the right diagonal edge so it lines up with the diagonal crease you just created.

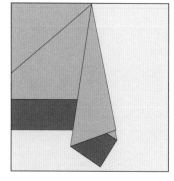

10. Fold over the right diagonal edge on top of itself again, toward the center.

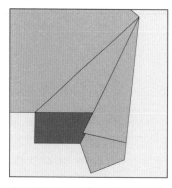

11. Fold the right edge over on top of itself a third time, again folding toward the center of the paper.

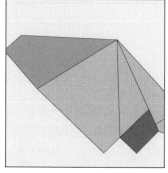

12. Repeat the folds on the left side. A protruding strip of paper will be on the underside, which you can use as a reference point.

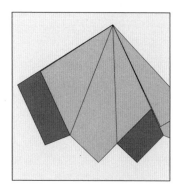

13. Starting at the top point of the center crease, fold down the upper point of the protruding strip to touch the bottom edge of the strip.

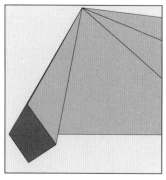

14. Fold over the left edge so it lines up with the diagonal fold you just created. Crease the fold.

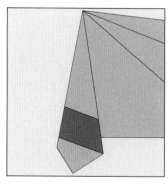

15. Fold over the left edge on top of itself again.

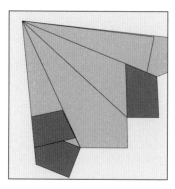

16. Repeat one final time, and your plane should look like the one shown here.

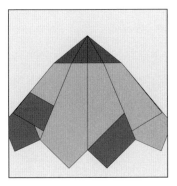

17. Fold down the tip of the plane's nose about three finger widths from the top. The top point must align with the center crease.

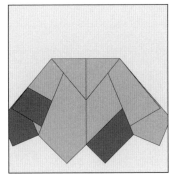

18. Flatten the fold—press hard so you crease all the layers of paper.

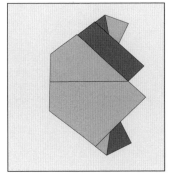

19. Flip over the plane and turn it so the nose points left.

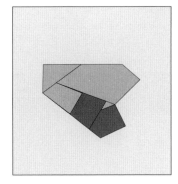

20. Fold the top wing of the plane in half downward along the center crease. Line up the wing flaps for good performance in flight.

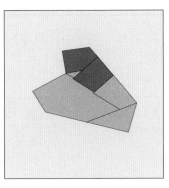

21. Rotate the plane so its nose points right.

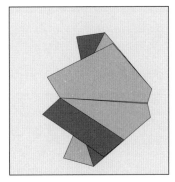

22. Fold down the first wing flap. Begin the crease at the nose about a finger width up from the paper's edge. Run the crease to the bottom edge of the paper.

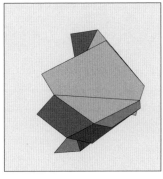

23. Crease the wing tip up. Start the crease's left point where the two layers of paper overlap along the back edge. The right point touches the right side of the center crease.

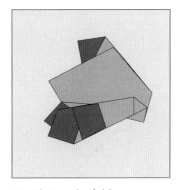

24. Flatten the fold.

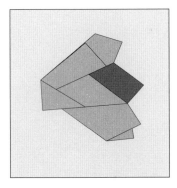

25. Flip over the plane and rotate it so the first wing flap is underneath and the nose points left.

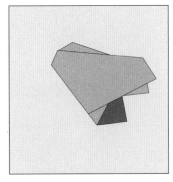

26. Fold down the second wing flap. Line up the wing flaps for good performance.

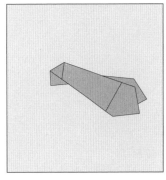

27. Crease the second wing tip up. Line up both wing-tip flaps so they're even.

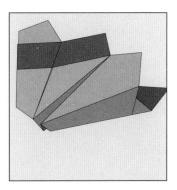

28. Open up the wing-tip flaps and the wings. Adjust so they're even on both sides for the most successful flight.

WILLOW

MODERATE

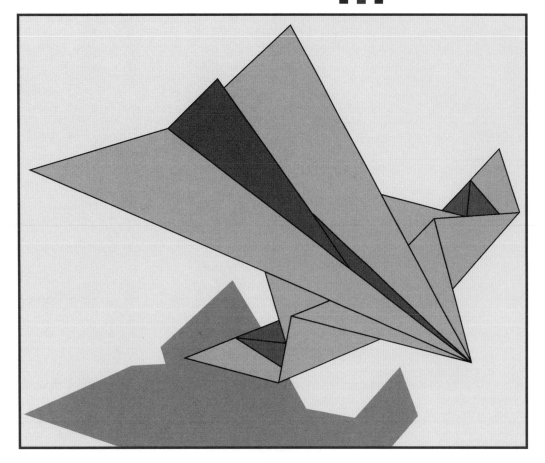

This craft offers real control surfaces near the nose, which allow an extra measure of experimentation in flight. Use medium- to heavy-weight letter-size paper for construction—while the nose folds look complicated, they're not particularly difficult to make. Launch the Willow with a gentle push throw. If the plane tends to float and stall, it's a sign that the creases aren't tight. Adjust the ends of the canards (the forward winglets) upward to improve performance. When the plane is trimmed well, you can throw it with greater force.

1. Fold down the upper left corner so it touches the right edge of the paper. The top edge of the paper should line up with the right edge. Unfold after creasing.

2. Repeat this maneuver with the upper right corner. After making a sharp crease, unfold the paper.

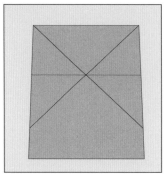

3. Flip over the paper and position it as shown. Fold down the upper corners to make a crease that intersects the center point created by the diagonal folds. Unfold.

4. Flip over the paper, keeping the creases at the top.

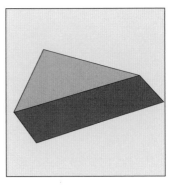

5. Pop up the ends of the horizontal crease and bring them toward the center. The top edge of the paper will fold over. Press the fold flat.

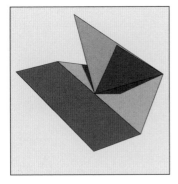

6. Bring the upper triangular flaps up from the base to get them out of the way for the next series of folds.

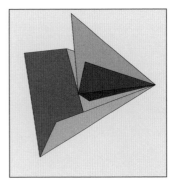

7. Crease the paper from wing tip to nose. The left point of the crease is at the lower left corner of the paper. The right point is at the tip of the nose.

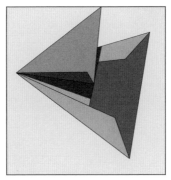

8. Turn the paper so the nose points left. Repeat the fold on this side of the plane, running the crease from the tip of the nose to the lower right corner of the paper.

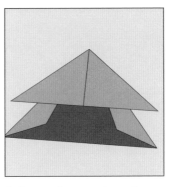

9. Lower the top triangular flaps over the folds just made.

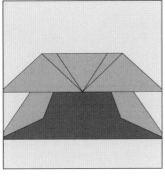

10. Fold the tip of the nose over and down to the bottom edge of the top flap.

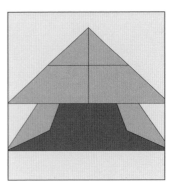

11. Unfold the crease.

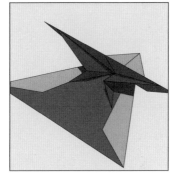

12. Pop up the top layer, bringing the left and right outside points toward the top. Also bring the inner points from the underlying triangular flaps up and out.

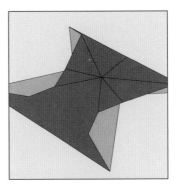

13. Press the fold flat to create two new creases.

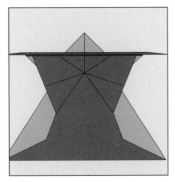

14. Fold the top flap in half downward.

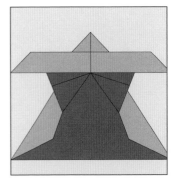

15. Make sure the new crease is parallel to the bottom edge of the plane.

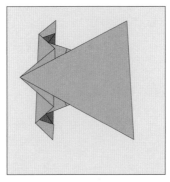

16. Flip over the paper and turn it so the nose points left.

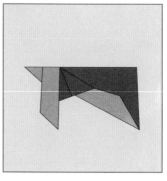

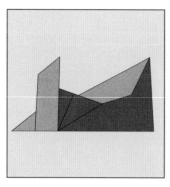

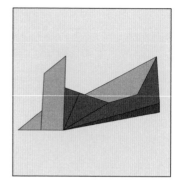

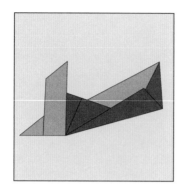

17. Fold the plane exactly in half lengthwise, bringing the upper portion down over the lower portion.

18. Flip over the plane so the bottom edge of the fuselage is down and the nose points left.

19. On the left, the crease starts at the forward canards. It meets the right edge of the plane about two finger widths up from the bottom edge of the fuselage.

20. Press the crease firmly so it's sharp.

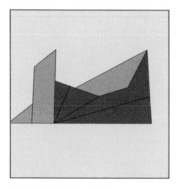

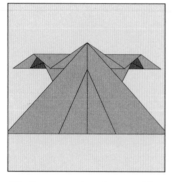

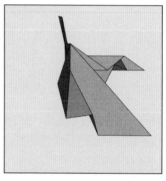

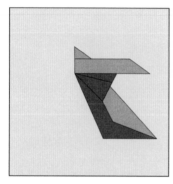

21. Unfold the tail crease.

22. Open up the plane and lay it flat on the work surface.

23. Reverse the center crease by folding it in the opposite direction. Then pop up the crease while folding the plane in half again.

24. When folded correctly, the tail section will tuck into the body of the plane.

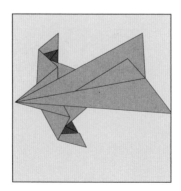

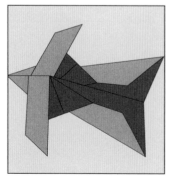

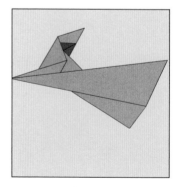

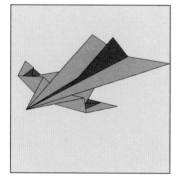

25. Turn the plane so the nose points left and the fuselage is down. Fold down the first wing flap from the tip of the nose to the lower back edge of the paper.

26. Flip over the plane, keeping the nose to the left.

27. Crease the second wing flap. Make sure to line up the wing flaps for good balance and flight performance.

28. Open the wing flaps and adjust the wing angles to be even. Set the dihedral angle level or slightly upward. Make sure the tail is straight and even and you're ready to fly.

CHESTNUT

MODERATE

This square-looking craft with real working canards starts out with some unexpected folds, making it moderately diffi-cut to construct. Launch this plane gently at a slight up angle or release it to float from a high place. For opti-mal flight, the Chestnut usu-ally needs some up elevator added to the tail corners to counteract the weight of the nose section. Bending the canards upward tightens them and changes the flight path even more.

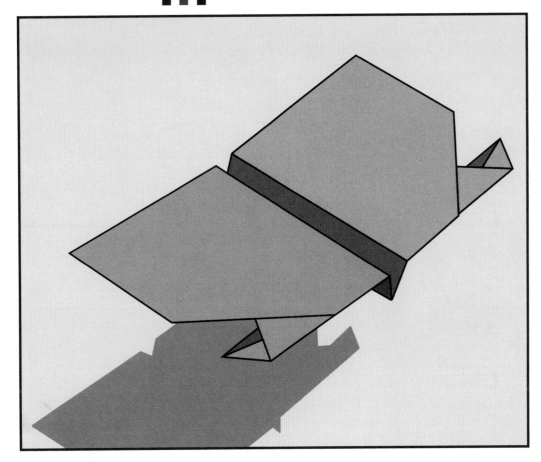

1. Make this craft with light-to medium-weight paper. Start with a letter-sized sheet.

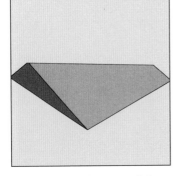

2. Fold down the upper left point so it touches the lower right point.

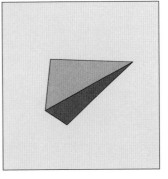

3. Rotate the paper so the crease is on the left. Fold the top point down so it touches the bottom point.

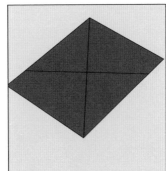

4. Unfold the paper.

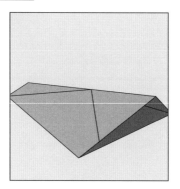

5. Rotate the paper so the upper point of the long diagonal fold is to the left. Fold the top point down so it touches the bottom point.

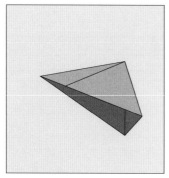

6. Rotate the paper so the new crease faces right. Fold the top point down so it touches the bottom point.

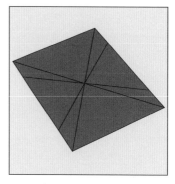

7. Once again, completely unfold the paper.

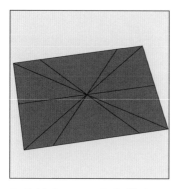

8. Fold the paper in half along its long edge. Unfold the paper after creasing and turn so the short end faces you.

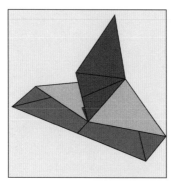

9. Folding over the upper diagonal creases on the paper's bottom half causes a mid-section flap to pop up. Two new creases form along the lengthwise crease.

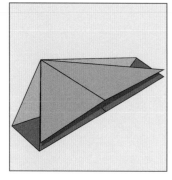

10. Split apart the layers of the flap, bringing the points out toward the lower left and right corners of the paper.

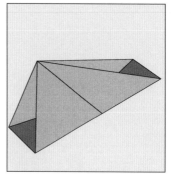

11. Bring down the point at the top of the flap to the center of the bottom edge of the paper. Press the fold flat.

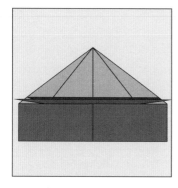

12. Fold the top-most layers of the paper over.

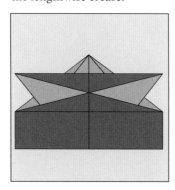

13. The left and right points of the new crease should be at the left and right points at the base of the folded triangle.

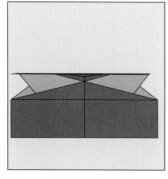

14. Fold down the nose tip to touch the center line.

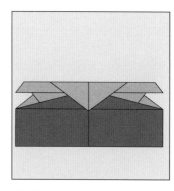

15. Crease the paper hard.

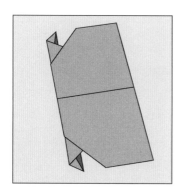

16. Flip over the plane and rotate it so the nose points to the left.

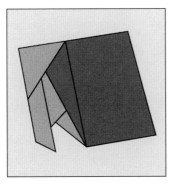

17. Fold down the plane in half along the center crease.

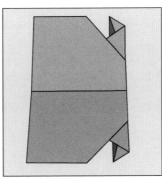

18. Rotate the plane so the nose faces right. Make a crease for the first wing by folding down the top flap.

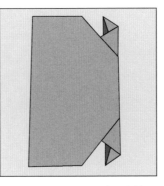

19. The new crease should be parallel to the bottom edge of the center of the plane and about a finger width up from the bottom.

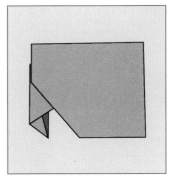

20. Flip over the plane so the nose faces left. Crease the second wing flap in alignment with the first.

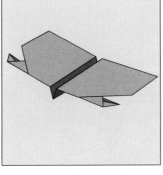

21. Open up the wing flaps and adjust the wing angles so they're even. Set the dihedral angle flat or slightly upward. Make sure the canards are tightly creased.

PRAY THAT IT WORKS

*T*he "praying hands" fold is commonly used in airplane production to establish the nose weight needed for good flight. Steps 9 through 11 of the Chestnut is a variation on the "praying hands" fold only because the crease angles are slightly different. The edges of the sheet come into the body at the same time to form an upright flap. This flap is then flattened against the body using the creases already on the sheet. Some of the creases will have to be reversed to make the fold correctly. This just means it will probably be easier if you pinch the creases in the direction they have to go before you make the fold. Make sure your plane looks like the picture before moving on. Once you've finished the folds, you'll find the craft finishes quickly and easily.

HICKORY

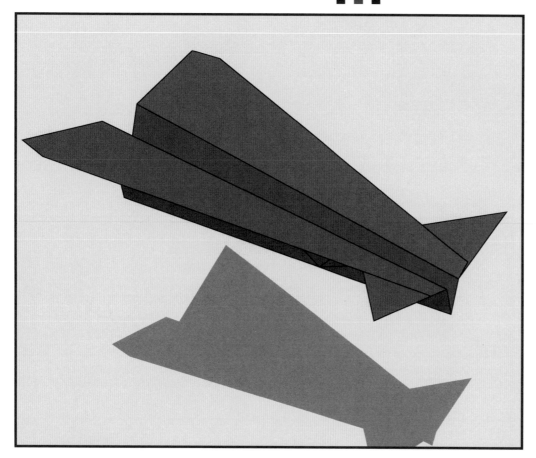

EASY

This sleek canard flyer is easy to fold from letter-size paper and great fun to fly. It's best launched level or at a slight upward angle with a moderate throw. This craft tends to float, but it is an extremely versatile flyer and can be trimmed to fly many different types of patterns. Try a piece of adhesive tape to hold the sides together, or adjust the canards way up or down for interesting flight variations. Make several—and feel free to experiment with them.

1. Start with a medium- to heavy-weight sheet of letter-size paper.

2. Fold the paper in half along its long edge. Unfold the paper after creasing.

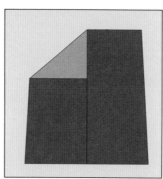

3. Fold down the upper left corner so the upper left point touches the center crease.

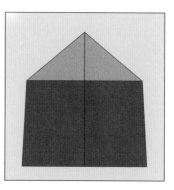

4. Repeat the crease on the opposite side of the paper.

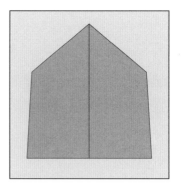

5. Flip over the paper, keeping the nose up.

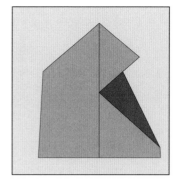

6. On the right side, fold a flap from the point along the center line. Press the paper hard to crease.

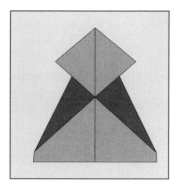

7. Free the flap tucked behind the fold.

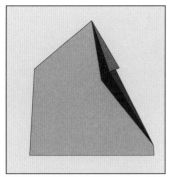

8. Repeat on the left side, releasing the flap that's tucked underneath.

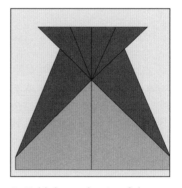

9. Fold down the tip of the nose so the top point touches the center crease at the point formed by the flaps.

10. Flip over the plane and rotate it so that the nose points to the right.

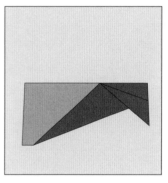

11. Fold down the plane in half along the center crease.

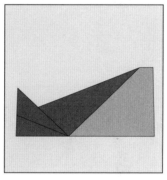

12. Turn the plane so the nose points left and the bottom edge of the fuselage is down. Fold down the first wing flap.

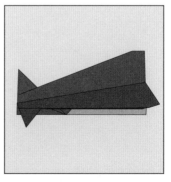

13. Angle the crease so its left point is a finger width up from the fuselage bottom and the right point is about three fingers up.

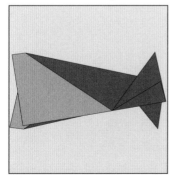

14. Flip over the plane so the nose points to the right.

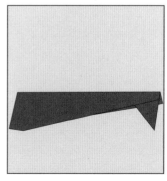

15. Fold down the second wing flap, lining it up with the first flap both for good balance and performance.

16. Open up the wing flaps and adjust the wing angles so they're even. Set the dihedral angle flat or slightly upward and you're all set to fly.

ZEBRA

MODERATE

This sharp-nosed fighter works best with light- to medium-weight paper. Most of the folds used to construct this craft are simple, but they can appear difficult at first glance. When in doubt, study the diagrams before proceeding with the next step. When constructed correctly, this plane is sleek and it's fast—able to fly at the highest speed of any of the fighters when launched with a hard throw. You can throw this craft at any angle, but watch out for spectators, since the nose is extremely sharp and could cause injury. If the plane spirals when flying, the dihedral is probably set too flat, so adjust it downward.

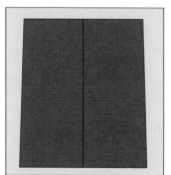

1. Fold your sheet of letter-size paper in half by bringing the long edges together. Make a sharp crease and unfold when finished.

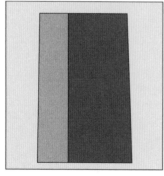

2. Fold the left edge over to meet the center line, creasing the paper sharply.

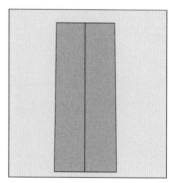

3. Repeat on the right.

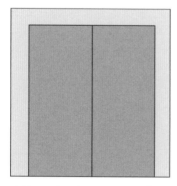

4. Turn the sheet over so the flaps are underneath. (The size of this picture is exaggerated for clarity.)

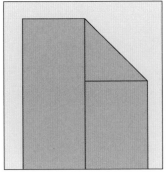

5. Press down the upper right corner of the paper, aligning the edge of the fold with the center crease.

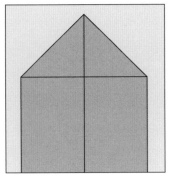

6. Repeat with the left corner.

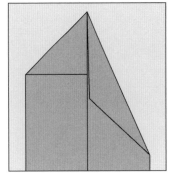

7. Fold down the right corner to align the edge with the center crease.

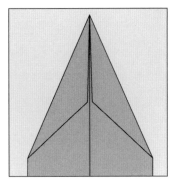

8. Repeat on the left side.

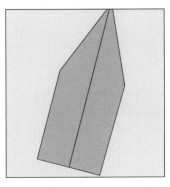

9. Turn the paper over so the flaps are underneath.

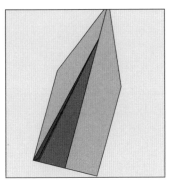

10. Open the left flap from the center. This will create a new fold.

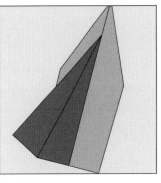

11. Crease a fold running from the lower left corner up to a point about three finger widths from the nose tip.

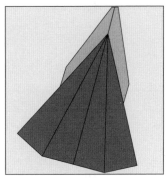

12. Repeat on the right, forming a new crease that runs from the lower right corner to three finger widths from the tip of the nose. Press the layers flat.

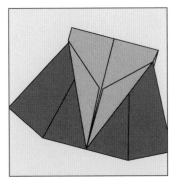

13. Fold down the nose to the bottom edge of the paper, making sure the nose touches the center line exactly. Crease the paper sharply.

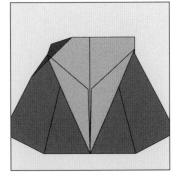

14. Bring the left corner over and down to form a new corner flap.

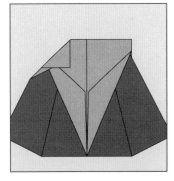

15. The top edge of the flap should be exactly vertical, parallel to the center line and about a finger width to the left of it. Crease the fold hard.

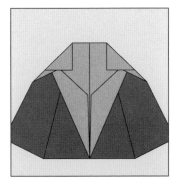

16. Repeat the corner fold on the right side, pressing down hard on the crease.

17. Pull up the nose, stopping when you touch the two new corner flaps.

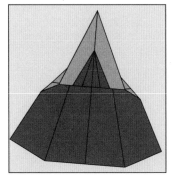

18. Make a sharp crease at this point.

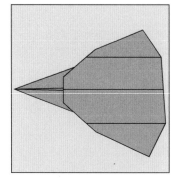

19. Turn over the plane and position it with the nose pointing left.

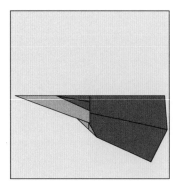

20. Fold the plane up along the existing center crease. If you folded everything evenly, all the edges will line up. Rotate the plane so the wing folds face down.

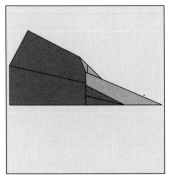

21. Turn the plane over so that the nose points right.

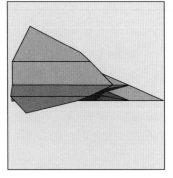

22. To make the first wing crease, bring down the top layers. The new crease should be about one finger width above the bottom edge and parallel to it.

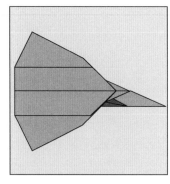

23. Press down on the layers as hard as you can.

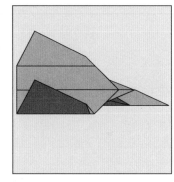

24. Bring the wing flap up, forming a crease along the flap on the top layer.

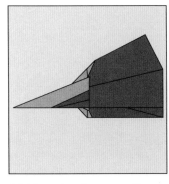

25. Turn the plane over from left to right. The nose should be pointing to the left. The main center crease should be at the bottom.

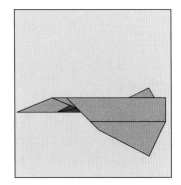

26. Bring down the other wing to form the second wing crease. Try to match the first wing crease as closely as possible for the best balance.

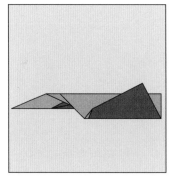

27. Bring the second wing tip up and crease along the existing flap line. Press down hard on all the creases. Now open the wings so you can adjust their angles.

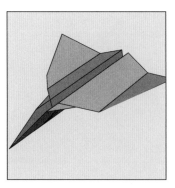

28. The dihedral angle should be set strongly downward at about 45 degrees. Angle the wing-tip flaps upward at about the same 45-degree angle, and the plane is ready to launch.

ANTELOPE

EASY

*T*his little airplane requires just one half of a square sheet of light- to medium-weight paper. Overall it's an easy craft to construct—the folds are tricky only because most of them are on top of each other. The nose section looks complex but is much easier to fold correctly than it appears. Launch the Antelope gently from a high place. When well trimmed, this little craft will float along easily. The front triangular section will tend to droop a bit during flights, but this should not affect the plane's slow, stately flying pattern.

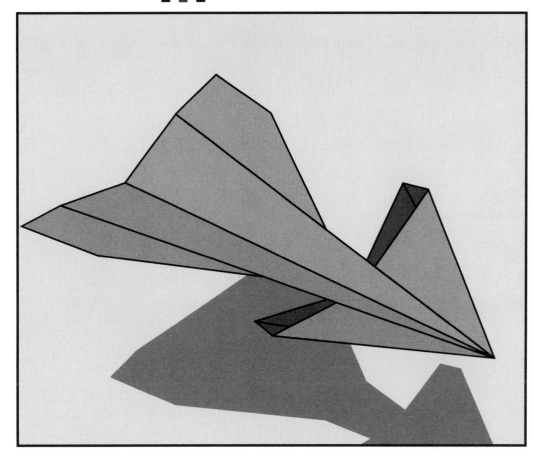

1. To start this plane, cut a sheet of letter-size paper square. Cut the square in half.

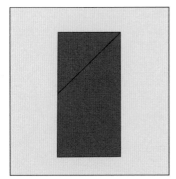

2. Fold the upper left corner over to the right edge of the paper. Make sure the top edge aligns perfectly with the right edge of the paper. Unfold after making a sharp crease.

3. Repeat on the right, bringing the upper right corner down and over to the left edge of the paper. Unfold after creasing.

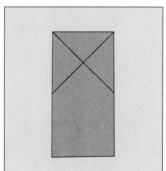

4. Turn the paper over, keeping the creases at the top.

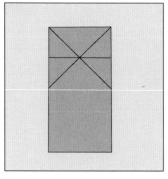

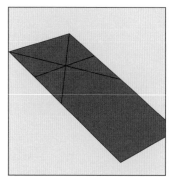

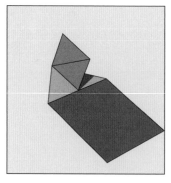

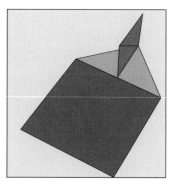

5. Bring down the top edge so the corners of the diagonal lines meet. This new crease should exactly intersect the point where the diagonals cross. Crease and unfold.

6. Turn over the sheet again, keeping the creases toward the top.

7. Bring up the two points where the last crease formed meets the edges. This pulls the triangles in and down to form a flap that stands straight up.

8. Position the paper to work on the right side.

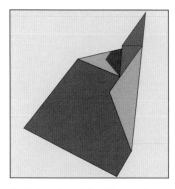

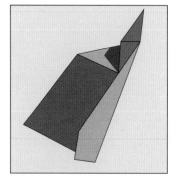

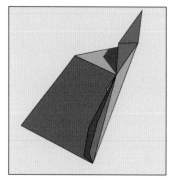

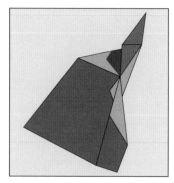

9. Bring the right diagonal edge over to the center line. It may be more convenient to lay the vertical flap down while making this crease nice and sharp.

10. Bring the diagonal edge of this new flap over to the center crease. As you did before, make this fold as sharp as possible.

11. Open the flap just formed to the right. The new crease should run from the base of the vertical flap to the lower right corner of the body.

12. Flatten the fold.

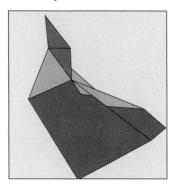

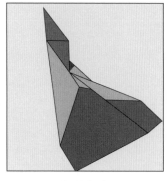

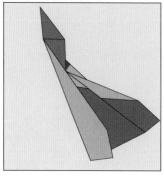

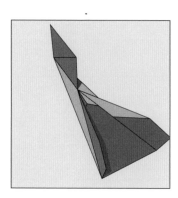

13. Reposition the paper to repeat the last three folds on the left side.

14. Bring the left diagonal edge over to the center line. You may wish to lay the vertical flap down while making this crease.

15. Bring the diagonal edge of the new flap to the center line. Press the fold flat.

16. Open the flap just formed to the left. The new crease should run from the base of the vertical flap to the lower left corner of the body.

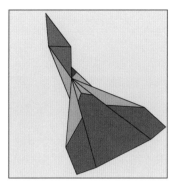

17. Make the crease as sharp as you can.

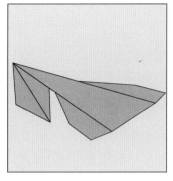

18. Turn the plane over and position it so the square flap is down.

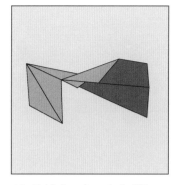

19. Fold the plane in half by bringing both wings up and forming the center crease. Line up all the edges before making this crease.

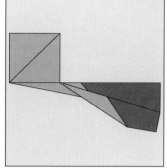

20. Turn over the plane and position it so the nose is toward the left and the square flap is toward the top.

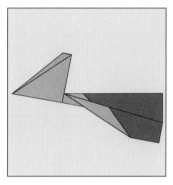

21. Bring the upper left corner of the square flap over and down to form a new crease. The left edge of the square flap should align with the lower diagonal edge of the nose.

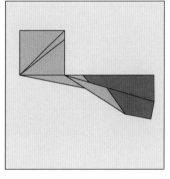

22. Unfold the crease that you just made.

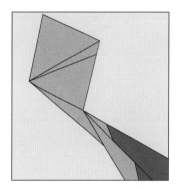

23. Reposition the plane to work on the square flap and the newly formed crease.

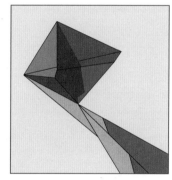

24. Open the square flap and bring it down upon itself. Fold both sides of the triangle down, bringing the new creases together on the underside of the plane.

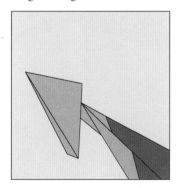

25. This will cause a small triangle to pop up in the middle of the nose above the body of the plane.

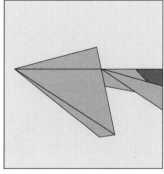

26. Reposition the paper and make sure your plane looks like the picture. Crease the triangular flap on top along the top edge of the body.

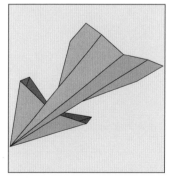

27. Open the plane and adjust all the angles so they're even. Set the dihedral angle upward and make sure the wing flaps are angled upward as well.

PAPER CUT

*T*o make the sheet needed for this plane, fold down the upper right corner of a vertical letter-size sheet so the top of the sheet aligns with the left edge. Cut off the strip of paper on the bottom. Take the square sheet of paper and fold in half. Cut along the crease.

ELK

MODERATE

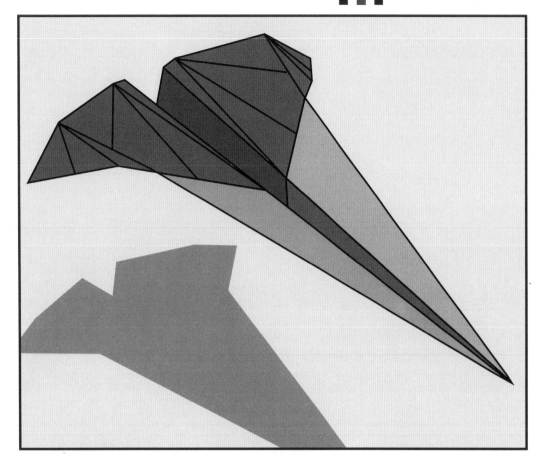

This dart-like fighter works best with a medium- to heavy-weight letter-size sheet of paper. Launch it with a moderately fast, level throw or at a slight upward angle. Flights with this craft range from dives and stalls to flip-overs, depending on the dihedral angle and the angle of the wing-tip flaps. Set the dihedral flat or slightly upward initially. Set the wing-tip flaps so they are vertical when the plane relaxes in flight. Don't be afraid to experiment to find the best combination of angles. You can change the flight pattern dramatically by attaching a little piece of tape to the fuselage.

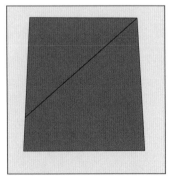

1. Fold down the upper left corner so it touches the right edge of the paper. When done correctly, the top edge of the paper will line up with the right edge. Crease and unfold.

2. Fold down the upper right corner in the same manner, so the top edge of the paper lines up with the left edge. Crease and unfold.

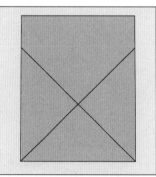

3. Flip over the paper and orient so the diagonal creases are toward the bottom.

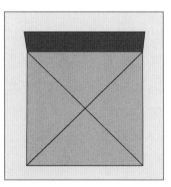

4. Fold down the top edge of the paper. The ends of the new horizontal crease should meet the top ends of the diagonal creases.

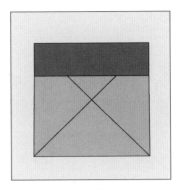

5. Flatten the fold.

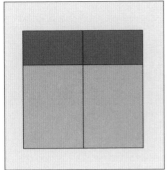

6. Fold the paper in half as shown. Crease and unfold.

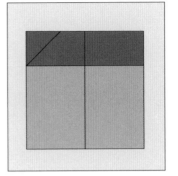

7. Fold down the upper left corner so it touches the bottom edge of the top flap. The upper left edge should line up with the bottom edge of the horizontal flap. Unfold.

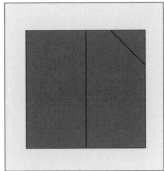

8. Flip over the paper.

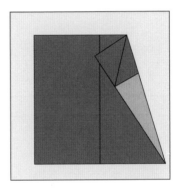

9. Fold the upper right corner. The bottom of the new crease should be at the paper's lower right corner; the top should be at the upper left point of the short diagonal crease.

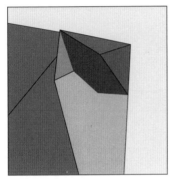

10. Pop up the bottom point of the top flap and swing it to the right of the paper while holding down the left edge of the flap. Press the fold flat.

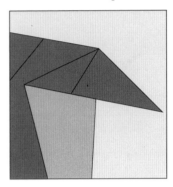

11. Be sure your plane matches the picture.

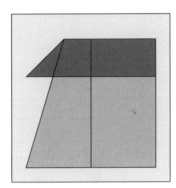

12. Flip over the paper, keeping the flap at the top.

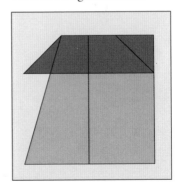

13. Fold down the upper right corner to touch the bottom edge of the top flap. The upper right edge should line up with the bottom edge of the flap. Unfold.

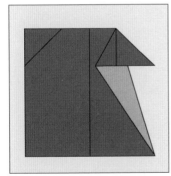

14. Flip over the paper.

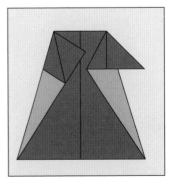

15. Fold the upper left corner. The bottom of the new crease is at the lower left corner of the paper; the top is at the upper right point of the short diagonal crease.

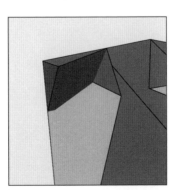

16. Pop up the lowest point of the top flap and swing it to the left of the paper. Hold on to the right edge of the flap as you do so.

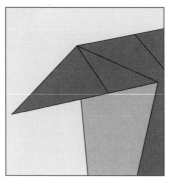

17. Flatten the fold.

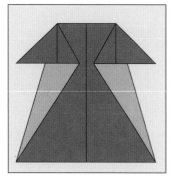

18. Be sure your plane looks like the picture.

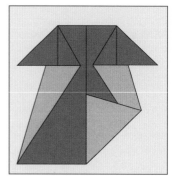

19. Fold up the lower right corner so it touches the center crease. The right half of the bottom edge should line up with the center crease.

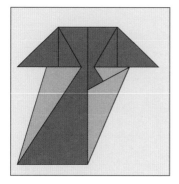

20. Fold in the point along the right side of the body so it touches the center crease. Make sure to line up the lower right diagonal edge with the center crease.

21. Pop up the top layer of the front triangular flap, bringing the point at the lower left over and down.

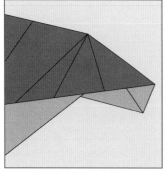

22. Flatten the fold. This will create two new creases.

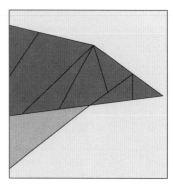

23. Fold over the small triangular flap so the lower point touches the upper right diagonal edge.

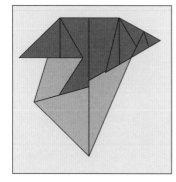

24. Fold the lower left corner so the lower left point touches the center crease. The left half of the bottom edge should align with the center crease.

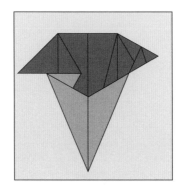

25. Fold in the point along the left side of the body so it touches the center crease. The lower left diagonal edge must line up with the center crease.

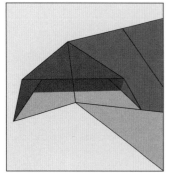

26. Pop up the top layer of the front triangular flap by bringing the point at the lower right over and down.

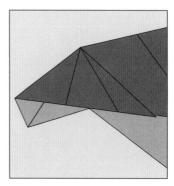

27. Flatten the fold to create two new creases.

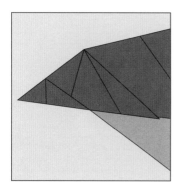

28. Fold over the small triangular flap so the lower point touches the upper left diagonal edge.

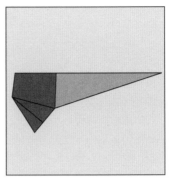

29. Rotate the plane as shown and fold it in half by creasing downward. Line up the sides for good balance.

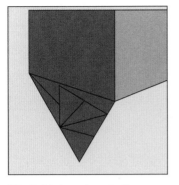

30. Fold the wing-tip flap. The size of this flap isn't too important, but aim for about a finger width wide.

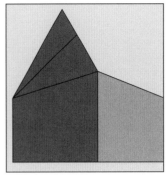

31. Flip over the plane so the first wing-tip flap is underneath.

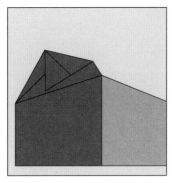

32. Crease the second wing-tip flap, making sure to line it up with the first.

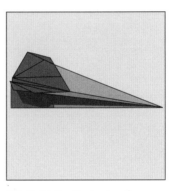

33. Fold the first wing flap down. The crease's right point is at the nose tip. The left point should be about two finger widths up from the bottom edge of the fuselage.

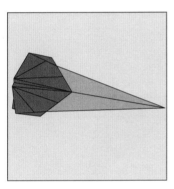

34. Flatten the fold.

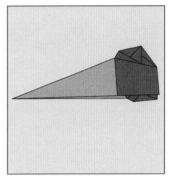

35. Flip over the plane and rotate it so the first wing flap is underneath and the nose points left.

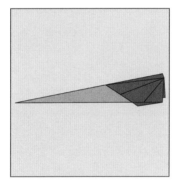

36. Fold down the second wing flap, lining it up with the first for good flight performance.

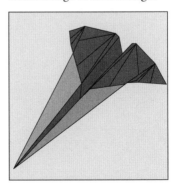

37. Open the wing flaps and adjust the wing angles so they're even. Open the wing-tip flaps and adjust to extend beyond the main wing flaps.

FLIGHT DIFFERENCES

*L*aunching this plane with the wing and wing-flap angles set upward will result in a gliding flight that stops in midair and drops to the ground. This is an interesting effect and is fun to play with because you can experiment with how accurately the plane will stop. For a straighter, quicker flight more reminiscent of military craft, try applying a piece of tape to the fuselage. Put the tape at the back of the plane where the two vertical parts of the fuselage come together.

CLIPPER

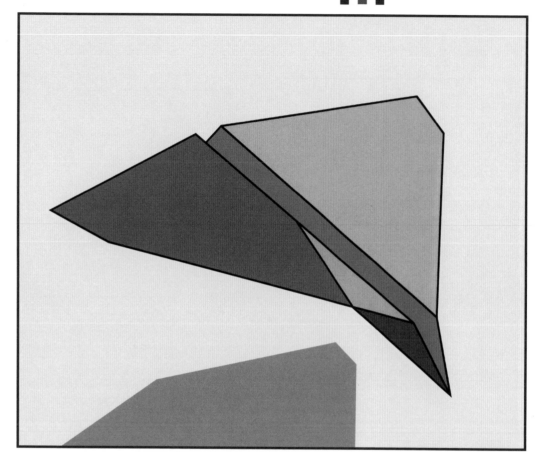

This easily folded little craft is fun to make and takes a minimum amount of paper to produce, so plan on making a lot of Clippers. Launch completed planes with a quick flick of the wrist at any angle. Greater thrust will make this plane fly straighter. When it's trimmed well, the Clipper should glide out straight after swooping and diving. If the plane flutters to the ground, it's a sure sign that the wing area is too large for the weight of the paper. If it dive-bombs directly to the floor, the wings are probably too small and the nose is probably too heavy for the weight of the paper.

1. Start with the strip that's left over from making a square out of a letter-sized piece of paper.

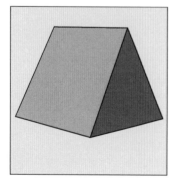

2. Fold the paper in half so the upper right corner meets the lower left corner.

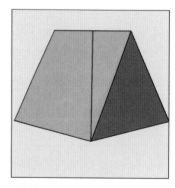

3. Flip over the paper, keeping the crease just created at the top. Then crease the paper in half along its long edge. Unfold the paper and flip it over again.

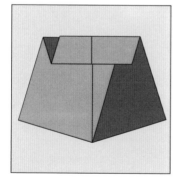

4. Fold down the top edge, keeping the middle crease aligned through all the folds. Make the fold about a finger width from the top. The fold determines the overall wing area so it may need adjustment.

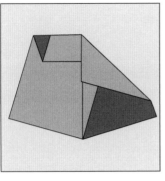

5. Fold down the upper right corner so it aligns with the center crease.

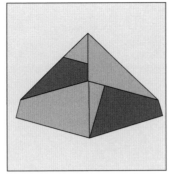

6. Repeat the fold on the left side of the paper.

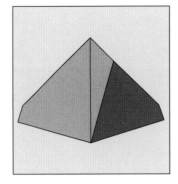

7. Flip over the paper, keeping the nose at the top.

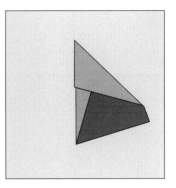

8. Fold the plane in half along the existing center crease. For good balance, carefully line up the wing flaps.

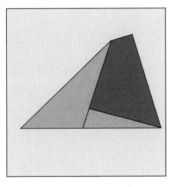

9. Rotate the plane so the wing flaps are up and the nose points to the left.

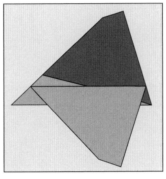

10. Fold down the wing flap parallel to the bottom edge of the plane and about a finger width up from it. The wing area can be adjusted by making this crease higher or lower.

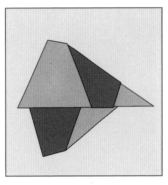

11. Flip over the plane and rotate it so the first wing flap is underneath and the nose points to the right.

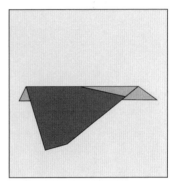

12. Fold down the second wing flap in alignment with the first flap.

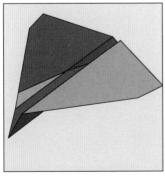

13. Open up the wing flaps and make the wing angles equal. Set the dihedral angle slightly upward, put an upcurl on the wings, and the plane is ready to fly.

TAKE OFF FROM A STRIP

To create the size of paper needed for this plane, you must trim a strip from a letter-size sheet. Position the sheet vertically and fold down the upper right corner so the top edge aligns with the left edge of the paper. Cut off the strip left on the bottom of the sheet and use it to make the microsize Clipper.

TRIREME

III

EASY

This zippy little plane is experimental, but it's very easy to build, so plan on making more than one. Start with a letter-sized piece of paper and trim it to a square, then make the plane out of the strip you cut off. When you're finished constructing the plane, launch it with a flick of the wrist at any angle you like. After swooping and diving, it should glide out straight if it's trimmed well. If the plane flutters to the ground, the wing area is too large for the weight of the paper. If it dive-bombs directly to the floor, the wings are too small and the nose too heavy for the weight of the paper.

1. Start with the leftover strip from making a square out of a letter-sized piece of paper.

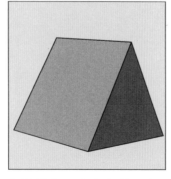

2. Fold the strip in half so the upper right corner touches the lower left corner.

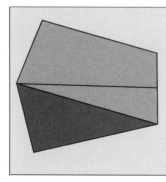

3. Rotate the paper so the fold you just created is on the right. Crease the paper in half along its long edge. Unfold the paper.

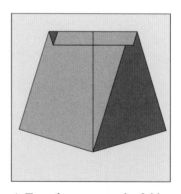

4. Turn the paper so the fold is at the top. Fold down the top edge about a finger width, keeping the middle creases aligned. The fold determines the wing area; adjust it up or down as needed in flight tests.

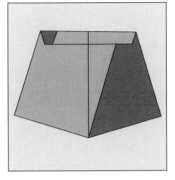

5. Fold the top edge over on itself a second time.

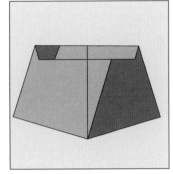

6. Fold the top edge over on itself one last time. Make sure all these creases are parallel to the top edge and are tight against the previous fold.

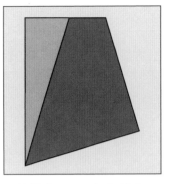

7. Fold the paper in half along the existing center crease. Line up the sides for good balance. Rotate the paper so the wing flaps are up and the nose points to the left.

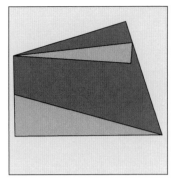

8. Crease the front wing tip down. The left point of the new crease should be at the upper left corner and the right point should be about one finger width down from the corner.

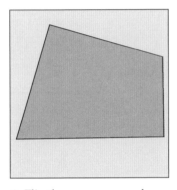

9. Flip the paper over and rotate it so the first wing tip flap is underneath and the nose points to the right.

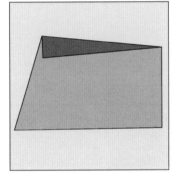

10. Make a crease to align the second wing tip with the first, making sure they're even.

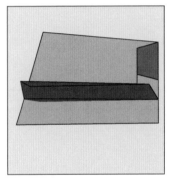

11. Fold down the first wing flap. The new crease should be parallel to the bottom edge of the fuselage and should be about one finger width up from the bottom edge.

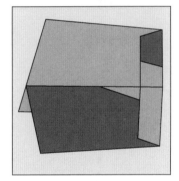

12. The wing area can be adjusted here by making the crease higher or lower.

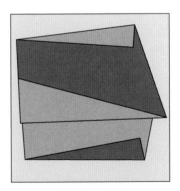

12. Flip the plane over and rotate it so the first wing flap is underneath and the nose points to the left.

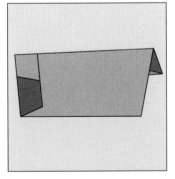

13. Crease the second wing flap. Be sure to line up the wing flaps for good balance and successful flight.

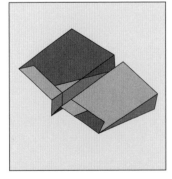

14. Open the wing flaps and the wing-tip flaps and adjust the angles so they're even. The dihedral should be flat or slightly up and the wing flaps should be vertical.

CUTTING THE SHEET

The strip needed for this plane can be easily created from a letter-size sheet. Have the short edges on the top and bottom. Fold down the upper right corner so the top aligns with the left edge. Cut where the right side meets the sheet and you're ready to start folding.

SLOOP

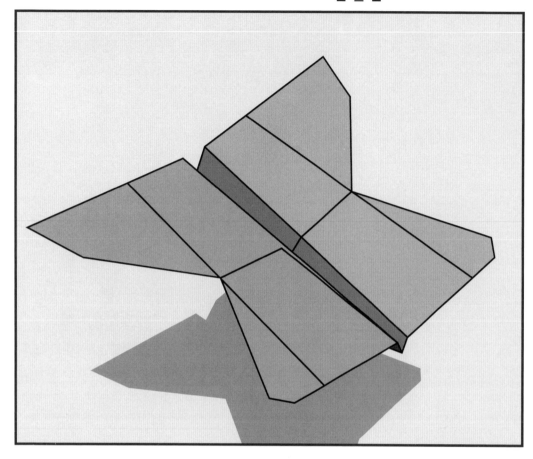

MODERATE

*T*he Sloop is a sturdy flyer and can be trimmed and flown in a variety of experimental ways. It has an appearance unlike any other airplane, but always flies when folded correctly. Launch with a moderate to hard throw at a slight upward angle. Since it's basically a glider, this craft tends to float and stall. You can reduce the wing area, and introduce flight-pattern variety, by making various flaps out of the front or back wing sections. Adjusting the angles of the flaps on the sides of the plane will also result in many different flight possibilities. With the right angle combination, it's possible to launch the plane and have it return to you.

1. Start with a sheet of medium- to heavy-weight letter-size paper. Fold it in half as shown.

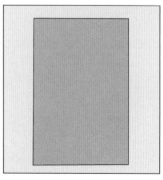

2. Rotate the paper, keeping the fold on the right. The paper should open up from the left-hand side.

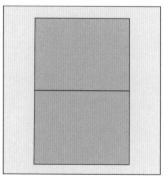

3. Crease the paper by bringing the short edges together. Unfold.

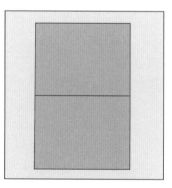

4. Rotate the paper so the fold is on the left and the paper opens from the right-hand side.

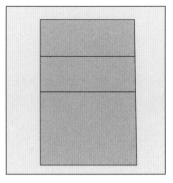

5. Crease the paper by aligning the top edge with the existing center crease. Unfold.

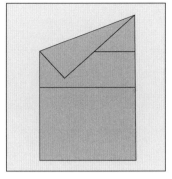

6. Fold down the upper left corner at the point where the edge intersects the crease.

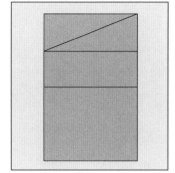

7. Unfold the crease.

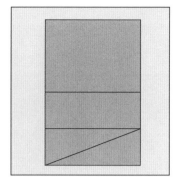

8. Rotate the paper so the creases are at the bottom.

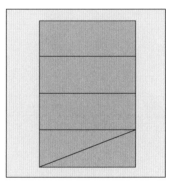

9. Crease the paper by aligning the top edge with the center crease. Make a sharp crease and unfold.

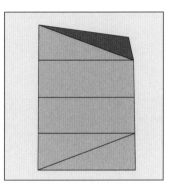

10. Fold down the upper right corner at the point where the right edge intersects the top-most crease.

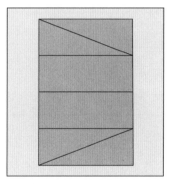

11. Unfold the crease.

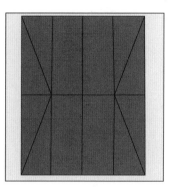

12. Unfold the paper and turn it over so that it's flat on the work surface.

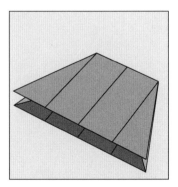

13. Use the angled creases to bring the diagonal flaps into the center of the paper. As you fold the sheet, bring the top edge to the bottom.

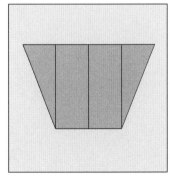

14. Rotate the paper so the nose is at the bottom.

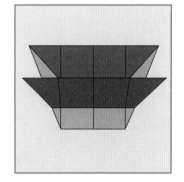

15. Fold down the top edge of the paper, making a new crease parallel to the bottom edge of the paper. Use the points of the interior triangles as a reference when folding.

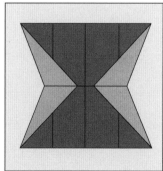

16. As you can see, the new crease should cross the innermost points of the triangular sections.

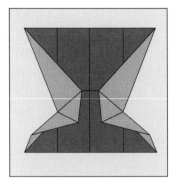

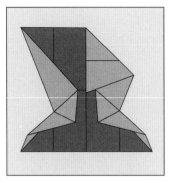

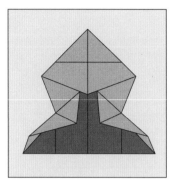

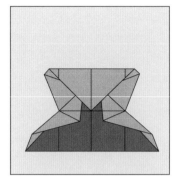

17. Fold the lower left and right flaps in toward the center as far as the paper will allow while still remaining flat against the work surface.

18. Fold over the upper right corner so the right half of the top edge lines up with the center crease.

19. Repeat with the left side.

20. Fold down the tip of the nose so it touches an imaginary line (shown in the picture) between the narrowest points on the plane. Make sure your plane matches the picture.

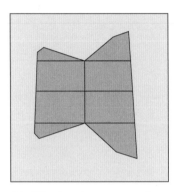

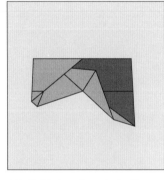

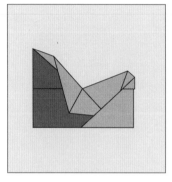

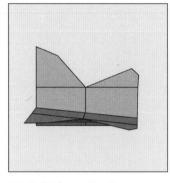

21. Flip the plane over and rotate it so all the folds are underneath. Point the nose to the left.

22. Fold the plane in half downward along the center crease. Carefully line up the sides for good balance.

23. Turn the plane so the wing flaps are up and the nose points to the right.

24. Fold down the first wing flap. The right point of the crease is one finger width above the fuselage and the left point is two finger widths up from the bottom.

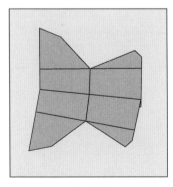

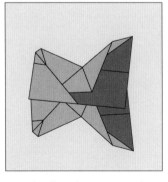

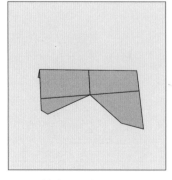

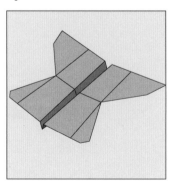

25. Flatten the fold.

26. Flip the plane over and rotate it so the first wing flap is underneath and the nose points to the left.

27. Fold down the second wing flap, aligning it with the first wing flap.

28. Unfold the wing flaps and adjust the wing angles so they're even. Set the dihedral angle flat to slightly upward.